Arrangiarsi

The Italian Immigration Experience in Canada

Essay Series 7

Arrangiarsi

The Italian Immigration Experience in Canada

Edited by Roberto Perin
and Franc Sturino

Guernica

Printed in Canada.
Antonio D'Alfonso
Guernica Editions, P.O. Box 633, Station N.D.G.,
Montréal (Québec), Canada H4A 3R1

Legal Deposit — 4th Quarter
Bibliothèque nationale du Québec & National Library of Canada.

Canadian Cataloguing in Publication Data

Main entry under title:
Arrangiarsi: Italian immigration experience in Canada

(Essay series; 7)
ISBN 0-919349-98-6 (bound) —
ISBN 0-919349-96-X (pbk.)

1. Italian Canadians. 2. Immigrants — Canada.
I. Perin, Roberto II. Sturino, Franc, 1948-
III. Series: Essay series (Montréal, Québec); 7.

FC106.I8A77 1988 971'.00451 C88-090064-4
F1035.I8A77 1988

Table of Contents

To our grandparents and parents,
migrants and immigrants whose itinerary
did not include wealth,
power and fame

Acknowledgements

We gratefully acknowledge the support of the following institutions and individuals whose contributions made possible the international conference entitled "Writing About the Italian Immigrant Experience in Canada" held in Rome at the Canadian Academic Centre in Italy: The Multiculturalism Directorate, Department of the Secretary of State, Ottawa; Ontario House, Paris; le Ministère des Affaires Intergouvernementales du Québec; the External Affairs Department, Ottawa; the Canadian Cultural Institute, Rome; the Ontario Heritage Foundation; the Social Sciences and Humanities Research Council; the Canada Council; Canadian Pacific Airlines; the Banco di Napoli; the Banca Nazionale del Lavoro of Canada; the Centro Scuola e Cultura, Toronto. Special thanks to Antonella D'Agostino, Anna Buiatti, Andrée Beauchamp, Luisa Lombardi. Our deep gratitude also goes to Adrienne Clarkson, Canadian diplomat extraordinaire.

We would further like to acknowledge the support of the Mariano A. Elia Chair in Italian-Canadian Studies at York University and the Multiculturalism Directorate for the publication of this volume.

Many people have contributed to making this book possible. Among others, we would especially like to thank Robert Harney of the Multicultural History Society of Ontario, Hédi Bouraoui, Shelley Hornstein-Rabinovitch and Gabriella Colussi of York University, David Homel, and Beatrice Virginillo-Corbo, assistant to the Mariano A. Elia Chair in Italian-Canadian Studies, York University.

Introduction

The Immigrant: Actor or Outcast

Roberto Perin

As an undergraduate some twenty years ago, I was looking for a topic on which to do my senior honours paper. My supervisor was Terry Copp, a man who has always shown a high degree of imagination and sensitivity to new areas of research. He had the excellent idea, and this before the era of official multiculturalism, that I should work on the Italians of Montreal. His suggestion quite frankly repelled me. In spite of the real methodological difficulties of such a topic, my attitude was determined more by a desire to study a question that was "central" to Canada's past. In my mind, immigrants fit the category of *la petite histoire*; they were peripheral to, if not outside of, history. They were too local, too ingrown, too atypical for one to make a meaningful statement on the course of Canadian history. The topic itself I felt would diminish the historian who undertook it. As a result, Terry Copp's suggestion remained unfulfilled.

My response was that of historians in general whose attitudes in turn reflected the lack of concern and compassion which the immigrant encountered from the moment he decided to leave his country of origin. Governments, Churches, unions, economic and cultural elites in both the Old World and the New paid little attention to this need. Only when the immigrant was seen as a means of achieving the goals of a particular interest group did he become the object of their concern. As a result, the immigrant became important to promote the political and economic interests of the Mother Country, or as a statistic in a Church's drive to increase or retain its following, or again as a problem threatening the ''British'' character of Canada, in both the political and social sense of that term. The focus here was not on the immigrant as a human being, but rather on the immigrant as a means to an end. It would be too easy in this context of generalized neglect to see him as a victim, passively submitting to nativism, class hatred, and exploitation. These of course were very real and at times assumed virulent forms, despite the often expressed sanctimonious view of Canada as a tolerant and accommodating society, as the land of opportunity. But they are only a part of the immigrant's experience, that part which was external to him. By continuing to view the immigrant as some kind of flotsam aimlessly and helplessly directed by the currents of history, we merely perpetuate the image of the various elites and of many later historians, that of the immigrant as outcast.

Fortunately, the immigrant did not wait for permission from elites and historians to take his place in Canadian history. He did so on his own terms, in so far as he had the means to do it. He improvised a strategy which was an amalgam of Old World culture and New World conditions in order to *arrangiarsi*. This term has come to mean more than "making do" or "getting by" as the Italian dictionary defines it. *Arrangiarsi* is used for example to explain contemporary Italy's huge underground economy which Prime Minister Bettino Craxi proudly included in a glowing assessment of his country's economic performance. In the past, this underground economy was considered by government officials to be outside the pale, something shady and illegal. But all of a sudden, it became respectable, a subject of serious investigation and even of boasting when it could be shown that because of it, Italy's economy was outperforming that of Great Britain. *Arrangiarsi* is also used to describe the widespread practice of tax evasion in Italy. It is the answer, usually accompanied by a wink, which businessmen and professionals give to explain their current economic status. The term encompasses all economic pursuits, not officially recorded or for that matter recognized, whether legal or extra-legal, to arrive at a subjectively defined standard of comfortable living.

Arrangiarsi is as much a reality of the immigrant experience as of contemporary Italy. Without the assistance of the governments of either the receiving society or the country of origin, temporary migrants and permanent settlers had to *arrangiarsi* to reach their targets for a decent life. They created networks among their own kind and thus skirted the moralisms and legalisms of the receiving society. They laboured in the shadows of that nether world, the fruits of which being difficult to quantify are the statistician's nightmare and, when the climate is right, the politician's pride. The term implies not the passivity inherent in the image of the immigrant as outcast, but inventiveness, quick-wittedness, forethought; in other words, activity. It does not mean that the immigrant is omnipotent or that he can fly in the face of those historical forces that are larger than he. But it does mean that he can turn those forces to his advantage. For example, Paul-André Linteau describes in his essay the historical roots of Quebec's inter-ethnic relations. The Italian immigrant had to insert himself into the world of French-English conflict. Given a context he could not change, the immigrant over time adapted himself to the dynamics of the situation and has learned to *arrangiarsi* in a peculiarly Quebec way.

Since the mid-seventies, Canadian historians have begun to reassess immigrant history in light of the experience of *arrangiarsi*. They discarded the traditional elite's perspective, the most easily accessible testimony of the immigrant experience up to that time, replete with stereotypes, common wisdoms, and generally well-meaning prejudices. They favoured instead an approach that tried to see that experience through the immigrant's eyes or from the bottom up, as the new social historians would have it. This approach is not of course the last word on the immigrant experience, since the perceptions of a group usually do not coincide with objective reality. But it is an essential beginning for understanding that reality. Robert Harney led the way in this process with a series of important conceptual studies which represented the immigrant as he really was, a protagonist.[1]

To grasp the historiographical transformation that has occurred in the last decade, one merely has to consider how the traditional elites and recent historians each depict the people and institutions central to the immigrant experience. Let us begin with the *padrone*. The 1904 royal commission on Italian migrant labour regarded him as a ruthless exploiter of his fellow countrymen and as a marginal criminal. The Canadian governing elite chose to point an accusing finger at him rather than at the Canadian Pacific Railway whose labour recruiting practices they broadly tolerated, not to say encouraged. In the chain of exploitation, who was the more ruthless? (In our eagerness to see Canada as the immigrant's land of opportunity, do we not tend to forget that these opportunities were at the very least reciprocal, indeed that they were far greater for well-entrenched business interests?) For their part, the Italian diplomatic and clerical establishment looked upon the *padrone* as a boor and an upstart who had somehow insinuated himself into a position which was rightfully theirs, of mediation between "their community" and the receiving society.

Harney was among the first to see the *padrone* as the immigrant saw him, a necessary but temporary ally.[2] Illiterate peasants unfamiliar with the language of industrial society, be it that of Milan or Montreal, needed a series of go-betweens in order to reach their targets. They realized that there would be a price to pay for these services, likely to be high considering their own lack of these specific skills, and that there were risks involved. The image here is less of a helpless victim and more of a wary consumer who knows that the *padrone* will charge what the market will bear. This image is reinforced by the fact that once the immigrant became more integrated into Canadian life, he would require these services less and less and eventually dispense with them altogether. Harney also portrayed the *padrone* as immigrant, an easy scapegoat for the prevailing racism of Canadian society, for the "mistakes" of Canadian corporate interests, and for the chilling class hatred of the Italian cultural elite. Probably more than most immigrants, the *padrone* had to *arrangiarsi*, skillfully manoeuvring between the needs of the migrant labourer, the

Canadian capitalist labour market, and other rival *padroni*.

Just as the traditional view of the *padrone* made the immigrant appear as a victim, so the boarding-house cast him in the role of an outsider. In either case, he was not part of the fabric of Canadian history. Benign racists, like the young J.S. Woodsworth and Charles Gordon, better known as Ralph Connor, saw the boarding-house as a symbol of all that was un-Canadian and despite the melting-pot rhetoric, their agenda was clearly one of assimilation. Popular social thinkers who smugly compare our apparent accommodation of minorities with the assimilationist ethos of the United States would be well advised to rethink their paradigms.

Connor's novel, *The Foreigner*, the title itself speaks volumes, depicts the boarding-house as the locus of social and sexual deviance, of filth, poverty, illiteracy, and general human degradation.[3] Only when the immigrant comes in contact with select Canadians, those all-purpose Mr. Cleans who obligingly scrub away every trace of Old World culture, is his redemption secured. In the process, he discards his festivities and celebrations, his religious beliefs and practices, his dress, his sometimes frivolous, sometimes aberrant behaviour in favour of sober, earnest, and purposeful living and manly religion (which is the one where the Pope is not master of his mind!). The bedlam of his daily life, caused by his earlier unwillingness to abandon his Old World ways, blossoms into an Anglo-Canadian Eden of tranquillity, order, and productivity.

Because the Italian cultural elite was largely drawn from the same class as these social gospellers, they tended to share their conception of the boarding-house. The notable difference, however, was that they considered the institution to be a blight on their representatives as well. Since

Canadians generally perceived Italian migrants as atavistically possessing all those un-Canadian characteristics described above, the shadow cast on the boarding-house by their behaviour would be sure to touch the Italian consulate, the church, and other respectable community leaders. This is why, as Nicoletta Serio explains further on in this book, Italian *prominenti* sought to transform the immigrant's grinding poverty into dignified indigence by removing some of the more unseemly aspects of immigrant life from public view.

Once again, it was Harney who insisted on seeing the boarding-house as a part of the economic strategy followed by migrants and immigrants to reach their targets.[4] What the cultural elites failed to realize is that while Italian peasants may have been used to sharing a living space with many others in the Old World, that they did so in North America did not indicate a desire to perpetuate a traditional lifestyle. In fact, quite the opposite was the case. Their aim was to become more self-sufficient and independent, including in matters of housing.

Harney and other historians have also seen the boarding-house as a cultural cushion which eased the immigrant's transition from the Old World to the New. The emphasis of this literature tends to be on the boarding-house as a reflection of the culture of the country of origin. Would it not be more appropriate to see this institution as an amalgam of the cultures of the Old and New Worlds, and logically as a singularly North American institution? While admittedly the immigrant ate familiar food and spoke his dialect in the boarding-house, is it not equally true that he was as likely to talk to his *paesani* about his work experiences in Canada, his impressions of the climate and of the people, his Canadian dreams as much as about his *paese*. And was not the boarding-house a centre for gathering and distributing information about conditions of work and life in Canada? If only Connor had known!

At some point, a number of migrants realized that their economic prospects would be better served in Canada, and specifically in Canadian cities, than in the country of origin. They settled in urban centres and formed ethnic neighbourhoods.[5] Canadian traditional elites merely saw these Little Italies as boarding-houses writ large, with all their attendant social evils. Ethnic urban enclaves were located in decaying neighbourhoods and turn-of-the-century reformers offered the same solution to the problem of slums as Connor implicitly suggested for boarding-houses: their eradication. Urban activists simply did not see these enclaves as a facet of the immigrant's temporary economic strategy. Living in the urban core provided him cheap housing, a convenient location to work and *paesani*, and possibly indifferent landlords, willing to turn a blind eye to his lifestyle.

The Italian cultural elite were painfully embarrassed by these Little Italies. While Canadian observers generally saw the ethnic neighbourhood as an accurate representation of the culture of Italy, Italians for their part expected that this should be the case, but realized that somehow its culture was not that of the metropolis. In their minds, Little Italies were parochial, backward, superstitious and thus mirrored not the high culture of the home country, but that of its remotest backwaters. Once again, the immigrant became an outcast: he was seen as too Italian by Canadians and too much of a peasant, and therefore un-Italian, by Old World commentators. As a result, both elites set about to provide the benighted immigrant with a culture cast in their own image.

It may be useful at this point in my chronology of the immigrant's experience, when he becomes involved in the process of settlement, to consider the thorny question of his identity. This slight digression can be justified for two reasons: the first is that identity is central to my theme of the immigrant as actor or outcast; the second is that a lot of drivel has appeared on the subject in the popular media and, with the notable exceptions of Harney and John Zucchi, even recent historical writing has tended to take the notion of identity for granted and has not clearly articulated its bases.[6]

It was of course totally unrealistic for the Italian elite to expect the immigrant to be a standard-bearer of bourgeois Old World culture. The first wave of Italian immigration to Canada occurred barely thirty years after the unification of the peninsula. In addition, as Bruno Ramirez so accurately observes in this book, peasants in the Old World had not had the opportunity to be socialized into the structures of civil society. Their lives were conducted within the bounds of kinship and *paese* networks which also largely defined the process of migration and of finding jobs and housing in the New World. Historical studies of North American Little Italies have shown how these networks were transferred to the New World and how as a result these communities were fragmented by *campanilismo*. Franc Sturino provides below a definition of the *paese* by exploring its physical and social limits. It is an important piece because the immigrant's identity was local and focused on the *paese*. Even the largely Southern Italian immigrants arriving after World War II, although products of liberal and fascist efforts at cultural homogenization, largely retained what Pier Paolo Pasolini non-pejoratively termed their archaic Mediterranean cultures.[7]

Needless to say, they functioned within the same networks as had the immigrants who preceded them earlier in the century.

In other words, the Southerner who became an immigrant had his own culture which was the only one he could preserve or retain. He could of course acquire another one (North American or Italian), but unless that acquisition were rooted in his every day experience, it would remain foreign to him. In this regard, Zucchi posits the emergence of a broader Italian identity, born of the Canadian experience of work, neighbourliness, and the defense of common interests. Voluntary associations emerged in late Victorian Toronto which broke down the barriers of *paese* and brought together immigrants as disparate as Northerners and Southerners.[8] This argument, however, must be qualified in some important respects. First, the new identity which emerged was not the metropolitan variety. The Italian consul general would have felt as uncomfortable attending a Toronto meeting of an association of moulders comprising immigrants from Friuli and Terracina as he would have that of a Sicilian confraternity. Because this new identity blossomed in the Canadian environment, it would be more accurate and less confusing to refer to it as Italian-Canadian, rather than Italian. Second, it is not at all clear, as Zucchi himself admits, that this identity superseded the older one based on *paese*. Indeed if the two coexisted, it would be interesting to try to determine which would have been dominant. Finally, one must distinguish between "Italian" organizations formed in specifically Canadian circumstances and those created by the elite to advance their interests. The culture of the first, I would suggest, was Italian-Canadian while that of the other was Italian. However we wish to look at it, the cultural life of

Italian communities in Canada varied considerably from the metropolitan model.

In moments of despair, the Italian cultural elite was even heard to say about the immigrants, "They are not Italians". In a sense, they were quite correct. Immigrants brought with them a pre-industrial, millenial Mediterranean culture which was largely circumscribed by family and *paese*. This reality is best expressed in the marvellous poem by Caro Cantasano, quoted in Susan Iannucci's essay which itself explores contemporary expressions of immigrant identity. The poem is entitled "My Grandfather Didn't" (i.e. didn't read Dante).

Over the past century, consular officials, clerics, and other *prominenti* have tried to shear away the immigrant's particularistic culture and in its place implant that of the metropolis. Their assumption was that he was an "imperfect" Italian who expressed a backward, and therefore inferior, form of culture and who needed the mediation of *prominenti* to turn him into a modern standard Italian. They advocated cultural persistence in the New World. However, they were not referring to the immigrant's culture, but to one which never existed in North America despite the creation of national parishes, the establishment of language classes for the children of immigrants, and the campaigns described by Harney in this book to raise the national consciousness of the community.

This point is illustrated by an 1887 Vatican report on Italian emigration, largely inspired by Giovanni Battista Scalabrini, bishop of Piacenza and founder of a community of priests dedicated to the care of Italian immigrants. The document bemoaned the Americanization of Italians in the United States.[9] It observed that nothing remained of their Italianness, but their name. The report suggested that the reason for this loss of identity was the fragmentation of the Italian community into so many regional subgroups and recommended the creation of "national structures," such as Italian parishes. These were intended to override the particularisms of the *paese* and ensure the preservation of Italian culture in North America.

We may forgive the author for his optimistic assessment of the cultural survival of minorities on this continent. In retrospect, he was clearly wrong. The history of immigrants in the United States and Canada in the last century has shown how problematical that survival was. This situation had less to do with nativism and the group's own will to survive and more with the reality of the immigrant's having to come to terms sooner or later with the English-speaking environment of North America. Despite this obvious fact, the Italian elite until recently continued to refer to their communities abroad as *colonie*. Yet the Italians who came to the New World were not settling in a virgin land as did the classical Greeks or in our own times, the French, English, Spanish, and Portuguese. They arrived instead in countries whose languages and institutions were already set. This did not mean of course that the prevailing culture would remain fixed for all time; but rather that, barring some major upheaval, that culture could not be replaced or fundamentally altered. This is the sense which the expressions "founding nations" or "charter groups" should have in the Canadian context. These terms do not confer a special status on the English and the French over other communities; they do recognize the historical fact that since the charter groups succeeded in establishing permanent colonies in this part of the continent, their languages and institutions must prevail.

The Italian traditional elite nevertheless expected

their immigrants who, it must be stressed, could not occupy a self-sustaining territory or establish indigenous State institutions to compete for their cultural survival with the charter groups. When we consider how difficult cultural retention has been for French Canada which is after all a nation with a far more complete culture (in the sociological sense) than any recent immigrant group, we may rightfully view the elite's expectations with skepticism, if not incredulity.

We cannot fault the elite for not being able to look into the future. Yet there is an aspect of this thinking which is worthy of blame, that is the failure to see that the immigrant had his own culture. This was due to a tendency to view Southerners with condescension. It is instructive in this regard that the above mentioned Vatican report recommended that preference be given to priests from the North for service to Italians abroad. This prejudice was of course commonplace at the time as it remains today among Northerners in general and the cultural elite in particular, many of whom view Southerners in quasi-racist terms.

But it must be stressed that the immigrant's culture could not, any more than some hypothetical Italian culture, survive intact in North America. The image of transplant which has been used to explain the persistence of ethnicity on this continent is not accurate.[10] It would be more appropriate, if we were to retain biological images, to speak of mutation. Context, after all, is sure to alter the form and meaning of behaviour. The Italian peasant is not the same person in the *Mezzogiorno* as he is in North America. It may be difficult for an outsider to assess this change since he can only observe that which is different from the North American norm. Not knowing the original context, he has no way of seeing how the immigrant's behaviour has altered in response to different circumstances.

Evidence of this change, while it exists, has not been systematically analyzed. We know for instance that the peasant's religious culture is very local, bounded by specific practices and beliefs some of which predate the advent of Christianity. Transpose these rituals to Toronto and something very fundamental has changed. The universe of communally accepted practices which was the foundation of the *paese* has been shattered. The immigrant may continue to cling to these rituals, withstanding archdiocesan pressures in favour of a more "rational" religion and the counter-rituals of rival *paesi*. But in the context of the secular city, his progeny will see these practices as folklore, that is mechanically performed rituals devoid of any significance, or worse yet, as superstitions to be discarded.

Language is another barometer of cultural mutation. The immigrant brings his dialect with him to North America and generally continues to speak it at home, at social gatherings, and because of the segmentation of the Canadian workforce, possibly at work. Over the years, however, that dialect undergoes subtle but cumulative changes, with the accretion of a wide number and variety of Anglicisms if the immigrant lives in English Canada and both of Anglicisms and Gallicisms if he is in Quebec. The dialect never changes to the point where the immigrant is no longer understood in his own *paese*, but it is sufficiently different to constitute a sub-dialect.[11]

Language is a reflection of the immigrant's altered identity. The hypothesis here is that his culture in North America is a curious amalgam of pre-industrial and advanced capitalist, of *paese* and megalopolis, of underdevelopment and affluence, those binary categories analyzed in William Boelhower's essay below. This is of course very theoretical and somewhat nebulous. To make this hypothesis more concrete, we need many more local studies which observe the immigrant experience in both its Old and New World context to assess what persists, what changes, what various forms the mutations take.

However varied that experience may be, it is clear that the immigrant's culture is a fleeting phenomenon. Like the religious rituals mentioned above, it is either retained as folklore by the second or subsequent generations or simply discarded as inappropriate behaviour. What is suggested here is not an assimilationist, but a true melting-pot model. The hypothesis underlying this model is that the culture of the receiving society has been altered by the arrival of immigrants on Canadian soil. In what ways and what new forms this change assumes is difficult to ascertain. It is clear, to cite a banal example, that Canadian cityscapes have been made more pleasant by the shops of Italian fruit vendors. By the same token, it is difficult to imagine that the Ontario government would have granted full public funding to Catholic schools without the large influx of Southern European immigrants to the province in recent decades. Beyond these concrete examples, we need more comparative studies on the Italian diaspora in the world, and especially in the Americas, to assess their cultural impact on receiving societies.

My discussion of immigrant culture suggests that if there were outcasts within the community, it was not the *paesani* (for allegedly failing to adhere to some metropolitan norm), but the elite who did not fit into the networks which formed the basis of that culture. For reasons of class, regional origin, or professional activity, these men were apart from the community. The nineteenth-century painters and sculptors whom Laurier Lacroix examines were Northern petty bourgeois whose patrons comprised the French and English-speaking elite of Montreal. It is true that they probably frequented the Italian church once it was established, that they ate Italian food, and hired Italian employees. Still, their lives did not revolve around kinship and *paese* networks for the simple reason that their own networks stretched out to the wider Canadian society. Their relationship with the immigrant community tended to be vertical rather than horizontal, that is they were in positions of authority either in the workplace, in the Canadian patronage structure, in consular bureaucracy, or in the Church. In addition, the further removed they were from that community, the more they tended to equate Italian culture with the metropolitan norm. Many assumed the mantle of cultural retention in order to enhance their visibility within the wider Canadian society as spokesmen, and therefore brokers, for "their community." As a result of this recognition, they consolidated their power within that community. What we know so far about the history of Italian immigrants in Canada suggests that that history is replete with instances of the elite exploiting the community in order to achieve their own narrow ends.[12]

Government officials might be well advised to reflect on these realities before drafting multicultural policies for various "ethnic" groups (the very term implies outcasts from Canadian life).[13] Are the advocates of cultural retention the elite or the immigrants themselves? What is to be retained, the culture of the metropolis or that of the immigrant? If it is the latter, this would seem to be difficult to achieve if one considers the evanescence of that culture. If it is the former, would it not be more appropriate to speak of cultural acquisition rather than retention? Certainly teaching our children more than two languages, as well as the histories of many peoples, is a laudable objective. Canadians, both French and English, have tended in the past to be insular: the first, concerned with their survival; the second, obsessed with mimicking the cultural forms of whichever metropolis controlled their destiny. Judging by the surfacing of nativism in Ontario over the heritage language controversy, we seem still today to be badly in need of having our cultural horizons expanded. But our objectives must be clear. If it is cultural acquisition we want, let us be rid of that rhetorical overlay of cultural retention which has permeated position papers, policy pronouncements, and political prattle for the past fifteen years.

In brief then, the immigrant was not some kind of amorphous lump of clay ready to be shaped by the *prominenti* into a perfect specimen of high culture. He carried with him a particularistic ancient Mediterranean culture which he proceeded to modify in response to his North American environment. In this process, as in others, the immigrant was a protagonist, even though he could not foresee the shape or direction of this cultural transformation.

The most important area of immigrant activity in North America was the workplace. The immigrant in general and the Italian in particular traditionally have been seen as reluctant to engage in the dynamics of the industrial system. They neither joined trade unions, nor participated in strikes or in working-class politics. Some historians even have considered them to be obstacles to the formation of a genuine socialist culture in North America. Ramirez shows further on in this book that such behaviour was not rooted in some atavistic peasant characteristic, but rather in the specific conditions of the Canadian labour market which offered the immigrant the dimmest prospects for improvement in the years prior to the Depression. Given these constraints from which socialist politics and trade unionism were far removed, the immigrant could only *arrangiarsi* in ways Ramirez very well documents.

Antonio Pucci gives us another picture of immigrants as workers when he deals with their experiences as navvies in the Thunder Bay area.[14] Confronted by the crude exploitation and repression of the big railway companies, these former peasants reacted violently and collectively, in ways which transcended *campanilismo* and even national boundaries. Pucci also indicates that Anglo-Saxon workers upheld trade union principles when it suited their narrow interests and that when their Italian colleagues were on strike, they were perfectly capable of scabbing. Angelo Principe, for his part, has chronicled the vicissitudes of the Italian anti-fascist and socialist press of Toronto, enterprises often operated by immigrant workers.[15] Between Ramirez on the one hand and Pucci and Principe on the other, which was the more typical immigrant experience? Many more studies are needed before a more complete picture can emerge.

Women are a vital part of the immigrant constituency. The traditional cliché of the Southern *contadina*, usually supported by foreign sociologists and anthropologists, was that of a passive, submissive, and conservative being. Two essays by Franc Sturino and Franca Iacovetta on the Italian immigrant woman in Canada have dispelled this caricature.[16] Working within the traditional constraints of peasant culture with its strict gender roles, women could influence, cajole, or dominate their husbands and thus be a power to be reckoned with within the family unit. They were actively involved in the decision-making process concerning emigration and at times determined it. Neither in the Old World nor in the New was their universe strictly circumscribed by the hearth. In the *Mezzogiorno*, their casual involvement in cottage industries among other things brought them into contact with a broader world. In Canada, their proportionately large participation in the active labour force after World War II provided additional opportunities to expand their horizons. The study of immigrant women is in its infancy, but already the *contadina* has joined her husband as an active participant in the historical process.

Generally, the immigrant experience has been one of material improvement, even if we cannot ignore the little-mentioned incidents of return migration and of mental and social breakdown.[17] It would be inappropriate here to begin a litany of rags-to-riches stories or indeed to blare out in triumphalistic tones a *Te Deum* to the great Canadian Earth-Mother for having suckled so well her adopted children. As mentioned above, opportunity is a two-way street: the immigrant certainly benefitted from coming to Canada, but so did those who exploited his cheap labour. In addition, we should bear in mind that the economic miracle which occurred in Italy in the 1960s has made the country cousin who stayed behind as affluent as the immigrant. Let us then leave smug phrases to the politicians and *prominenti* and focus instead on the lack of studies concerning the immigrant's social mobility, upward or downward.

What we have in this area is fragmentary indeed. Ramirez suggested that, in the period prior to the Depression, the immigrant's ability to develop co-operative strategies based on family and kinship structures avoided his having to rely on the marketplace to obtain some basic necessities.[18] In an article on the farm labour system in Ontario in the twenties, Sturino showed among other things how some fruit and vegetable merchants in the 1920s became wealthy by exercising a vital role of mediation between the supply of migrant workers from Italy and the needs of the Canadian labour market for casual farm labour.[19]

The above studies are in themselves very valuable. However at some point, these snap-shots of mobility have to be quantified to obtain not merely impressionistic accounts, but an accurate picture of social mobility. It is here that looking at the immigrant experience from the inside has to mesh with the broader Canadian reality. We cannot begin to understand that experience if we see it through any other eyes but the immigrant's. By the same token if we do not set that experience in the larger Canadian context, the immigrant will somehow still remain an outsider. This is a difficult and long-term task whose successful execution depends as well on the maturation and sophistication of Canadian social history in general, since the shortcomings of immigrant history necessarily reflect those of Canadian social history.

The preceding pages have already indicated further areas of research. More attention must be given to the immigrant experience outside Montreal and Toronto. Both in the present volume and elsewhere, Gabriele Scardellato has pioneered the study of Italians in British Columbia.[20] Antonio Pucci and John Potestio are focusing their research efforts on Thunder Bay.[21] A little-known, but solid monograph looked at the Italians of Timmins.[22] But silence largely shrouds the communities that developed out of the extractive industries in Cape Breton, north-eastern Ontario, and the Rockies, out of manufacturing centres such as Hamilton and the towns of southwestern Ontario, out of urban centres such as Ottawa and Winnipeg.[23] The importance of linking these New World communities with the Old through *paese* networks cannot be stressed enough. In this regard, Mauro Peressini's study of the Friulians of Montreal breaks new ground because it focuses on a Northern Italian group which has been largely neglected.[24] Studies of migrations from the *paesi* of Sicily, Puglia, southern Lazio/northern Campania, and the Abruzzi still await their authors. Franca Iacovetta has lifted the veil on the Italian immigrant woman. But she would be the first to acknowledge that her study of the Southern *contadina* in Toronto after World War II is the beginning of a process which must move back in time and outward in space. It should be noted that the last-mentioned studies concentrate on the post-1945 period, a welcome break from the heavy emphasis on the years of the first wave of Italian immigration.[25]

The stress, however, should not be on what remains to be done, but what has been accomplished in the last dozen years. It would not be an exaggeration to say that the breakthrough that has occurred in immigrant history in Canada originated in the pioneering studies on the Italian immigrant experience. The field which previously was more akin to museology, folklore, and genealogy was transformed overnight into a living historical reality.

It was in this context and that of the contemporaneous burgeoning of writers of Italian background that an international conference was held at the Canadian Academic Centre in Rome. Entitled "Writing about the Italian Immigrant Experience in Canada," the four-day event saw the participation of historians, literary critics, anthropologists, writers, photographers, film-makers, publishers from French and English Canada, Italy, and the United States. The purpose of this gathering was to bring together the various strands and personalities of what might be termed the flowering of Italo-Canadian writing. The results of the conference amply fulfilled expectations as collaborative projects of the interdisciplinary, cross-cultural, and trans-Atlantic type have mushroomed since then.

Organizing the event became a veritable adventure in *arrangiarsi*. Encouragement came quickly, enthusiastically, and generously from an immigrant, not I hasten to add of Italian origin, who happened to be Agent General of Ontario in Paris. Reaction from other quarters tended to be much less warm, indeed verged at times on outright hostility. The immigrant, it seems, remains an outcast, even when he is the subject of a conference.

Emigration and the fate of emigrant communities abroad are topics which on the whole leave the Italian public completely indifferent. The lack of response of Italians to the conference amply bore out this observation. The Italian national broadcasting network covered the event, but significantly it did so through its overseas service, the implication being that only the country of emigrant destination could be interested in the phenomenon of immigration. Yet at the same time, Italian newspapers were replete with stories about Mario Cuomo and Geraldine Ferraro, including anecdotes about ancient great-aunts reminiscing about them or their parents scampering through the streets of the *paese*. This shows that the immigrant is doubly victimized: he is the object either of indifference or condescension and folklorization by both the countries of origin and of adoption.

The "leadership" of Italian communities in Canada is notoriously anti-intellectual. When approached to support the conference either morally or financially, they were perplexed. They did not know what to make of the event since it could not advance their personal, economic, or political interests. They exhibited the attitude that what did not come from them could not exist. Therefore, they ignored it and missed the opportunity of participating in the first serious intellectual endeavour involving academics and writers of Italian origin from across Canada. The *prominenti*'s apathy and their ignorance underscores what has been said above about the traditional role of this group vis à vis the immigrant community.

Finally, the attitude of some "charter" Canadians to the event is also enlightening. Some expressed fears that the conference would stress an inordinate identification with Italy. Like latter-day Ralph Connors, they would have preferred participants to bleach away every trace of their immigrant origins and shine forth instead as whitewashed Canadians. Others were concerned that an emphasis on Italianness would arouse interest in ideologies acceptable in Italy but not in Canada. Make them Canadians, the Rev. A. Fitzpatrick, founder of Frontier College, said at the turn of the century, so that they will become Lincolns and not Lenins (the choice of characters is in itself instructive). Echoing this attitude, a government department even asserted to conference organizers that it could not pay for the travel expenses of Italo-Canadian poets because they did not qualify under its programme of support for Canadian authors! Attempts were even made to exploit the organization of the conference to advance political objectives. *Le plus ça change*...

Despite these setbacks, the organizers, through their own networks (this time not based on the *paese*), but personal, political, and governmental, succeeded in staging the event. What is presented here is a selection of historical and thematic papers from the conference. *Arrangiarsi* is a testimony to the endurance of immigrants.

NOTES

1. R. Harney, "The Commerce of Migration," *Canadian Ethnic Studies* IX, 1 (1977) 42-53; "Men Without Women," in B. Caroli, R. Harney, L. Tomasi, eds., *The Immigrant Woman in North America* (Toronto, 1978), 79-101.

2. R. Harney, "The Padrone and the Immigrant," *The Canadian Review of American Studies* V, 2 (Fall 1974), 101-18; "Montreal's King of Labour: A Case Study of Padronism," *Labour/Le Travailleur* IV (1979), 57-84; "The Padrone System and Sojourners in the Canadian North, 1885-1920," in G. Pozzetta, ed., *Pane e Lavoro: The Italian American Working Class* (Toronto, 1980), 119-37. See also B. Ramirez and M. Del Balso, *The Italians of Montreal, from Sojourning to Settlement, 1900-1921* (Montreal, 1980); B. Ramirez, *Les premiers Italiens de Montréal. L'origine de la Petite Italie au Québec* (Montréal, 1984).

3. Ralph Connor, *The Foreigner* (Toronto, 1909), also published in the United Kingdom and the United States as *The Settler. A Tale of the Saskatchewan* (London and New York, 1909). See also R. Harney, "Italophobia: English-speaking Malady?" *Studi emigrazione* XXII, 77 (March 1985), 6-43.

4. R. Harney, "Boarding and Belonging," *Urban History Review* II (1978), 8-37.

5. R. Harney, "Toronto's Little Italy, 1885-1954," in R. Harney and V. Scarpaci, eds., *Little Italies in North America* (Toronto, 1981), 41-62; "Ambiente and Social Class in North American Little Italies," *Canadian Review of Studies in Nationalism* II, 2 (1975), 208-24. John Zucchi, *The Italian Immigrants in St. John's Ward, 1875-1915* (Toronto, 1981); "Occupations, enterprise and migration chain: the fruit traders from Termini Imrese in Toronto, 1900-1930," *Studi emigrazione* XXII, 77 (March 1985), 68-80. B. Ramirez, *Les premiers*.

6. John Zucchi, "Italian Hometown Settlements and the Development of an Italian Community in Toronto, 1875-1935," in R. Harney, ed., *Gathering Place: Peoples and Neighbourhoods of Toronto* (Toronto, 1985), 121-46. R. Harney, "Chiaroscuro, Italians in Toronto, 1885-1915," *Italian Americana* I, 2 (1975), 142-67.

7. Pier Paolo Pasolini, *Lettere luterane* (Torino, 1980).

8. Zucchi, "Italian Hometown."

9. R. Perin, "Religion, Ethnicity and Identity: Placing the Immigrant Within the Church," in W. Westfall and L. Rousseau, eds., *Religion/Culture. Comparative Canadian Studies/Études canadiennes comparées*, special issue of *Canadian Issues* (1985), 212-29.

10. R. Vecoli, "Contadini in Chicago: A Critique of *The Uprooted*," *Journal of American History* LI (1964). For a different view, see F. Sturino, "Family and Kin Cohesion among South Italian Immigrants in Toronto," in Caroli, *The Immigrant Woman*, 288-311.

11. Marcel Danesi, "Ethnic Languages and Acculturation: the Case of the Italo-Canadians," *Canadian Ethnic Studies* XVII, 1 (1985), 98-104.

12. R. Perin, "Conflits d'identité et d'allégeance: la propagande du consulat italien à Montréal dans les années trente," *Questions de culture* 2 (1982), 81-102, also published as "Making Good Fascists and Good Canadians: Consular Propaganda and the Italian Community in Montreal in the 1930s," in G. Gold, ed., *Minorities and Mother Country Imagery* (St. John's, 1984), 136-58. L. Bruti Liberati, "Le relazioni tra Italia e Canada e l'emigrazione italiana nel primo Novecento," *Studi emigrazione* XXII, 77 (March 1985), 44-66; *Il Canada, l'Italia e il fascismo, 1919-1945* (Rome, 1984).

13. For an assessment of Canadian multicultural policy, see the article with the unlikely title by R. Harney, "Ethnic Archival and Library Materials in Canada: Problems of Bibliographic Control and Preservation," *Ethnic Forum: Journal of Ethnic Studies and Ethnic Bibliography* 2, 2 (Fall 1982), 3-31.

14. A. Pucci, "Canadian Industrialization versus the Italian Contadini in a Decade of Brutality, 1902-1912," in Harney and Scarpaci, *Little Italies*, 182-207.

15. A. Principe, "The Italo-Canadian Press of Toronto, 1922-1940," Italian Section/Northeast Modern Languages Association Conference, *Proceedings* IV (1980), 119-37.

16. F. Sturino, "The Role of Women in Italian Immigration to the New World," in J. Burnet, ed., *Looking into My Sister's Eyes: an Exploration in Women's History* (Toronto, 1982), 21-32. F. Iacovetta, "From Contadina to Worker: Southern Italian Working Women in Toronto, 1947-1962," in Burnet, *Looking into*, 195-222.

17. In F. Sturino, "The Social Mobility of Italian Canadians: 'Outside' and 'Inside' Concepts of Mobility," in F. Sturino and J. Zucchi, eds., *Italians in Ontario*, special issue of *Polyphony* 7, 2 (Fall-Winter 1985), 123-27. The author makes an intelligent plea to social scientists to take into account Old World skills and status as well as the socio-historical context at the time of entry into Canada when trying to assess the social status and mobility patterns of specific ethnic groups.

18. B. Ramirez, "Montreal's Italians and the Socio-Economy of Settlement, 1900-1930: Some Historical Hypotheses," *Urban History Review* X, 1 (June 1981), 39-48.

19. F. Sturino, "Italian immigration to Canada and the farm labour system through the 1920's," *Studi emigrazione* XXII, 77 (March 1985), 81-97.

20. G. Scardellato, "Italian Immigrant Workers in Powell River, B.C.: A Case Study of Settlement Before World War II," *Labour/Le Travail* 16 (Fall 1985), 145-63.

21. J. Potestio, "Le memorie di Giovanni Veltri: da contadino a impresario di ferrovia," *Studi emigrazione* XXII, 77 (March 1985), 129-139; a shorter English version was published as "The Memoirs of Giovanni Veltri," in Sturino and Zucchi, *Italians in Ontario*, 14-19.

22. J.L. DiGiacomo, *They Live in the Moneta: an Overview of the History and Changes in Social Organization of Italians in Timmins, Ontario* (Downsview, Ont. 1982).

23. The special issue of *Polyphony* 7, 2 (Fall-Winter 1985) edited by F. Sturino and J. Zucchi and entitled *Italians in Ontario* has broken new ground in this regard. See

especially, Enrico Cumbo, "Italians in Hamilton, 1900-1940," 28-36; Walter Temelini, "The Italians in Windsor," 73-80.

24. Mauro Peressini, "Stratégies migratoires et pratiques communautaires: les Italiens du Frioul" *Recherches sociographiques* XXV, 3 (septembre-décembre 1984), 367-91.

25. See in this regard, R. Harney, "How to Write a History of Post-War Toronto Italia," in Sturino and Zucchi, *Italians in Ontario*, 61-66. F. Sturino, "Post-World War Two Canadian Immigration Policy towards Italians," in Sturino and Zucchi, *Italians in Ontario*, 67-72; "A Case Study of a South Italian Family in Toronto, 1935-1960," *Urban History Review* II (1978), 38-57.

THE REGIONS OF ITALY

Caboto and Other *Parentela*: The Uses of the Italian-Canadian Past

Robert F. Harney

Frantz Fanon, observing the feverish use and abuse of history practised by both sides in the Algerian struggle for independence, came to understand the significance of the past as a legitimizer of status in the present. "While the politicians situate their action in actual present day events," he wrote, "men of culture take their stand in the field of history."[1] Ethnic history, as the story of each people's participation in the development of North America, has also become a weapon in the individual and group struggle to "make it" in the United States and Canada. Because the battle for status in North America has insidious impact on the writing of history, we must look at some problems of how Italian North Americans perceive their history, especially their mass migration from Italy and their role in civilizing the Western Hemisphere.

The manipulation of the past to create a pedigree in the present is not unique to any one ethnic group. That it happens at all is the consequence of the rather understandable but mistaken assumption that ethnic group status in North America and thus, at least partly, the individual's own sense of eth-class, derives from notions of being "long in the land" and of respectability. In its American form, called "Mayflowerism," such uses of history have long been a device of the Old Stock, of those from the British Isles and northwestern Europe, to justify their ethnocultural hegemony. In Canada the problem is given official status in the concept of "the founding nations," which claims a special place for the French and anglophone groups, even within the context of multiculturalism.

The response to the Old Stock's assertion of privilege has been a spate of counter-claims. Italian North Americans have participated in this unseemly race to establish respectability and roots in the land. One Italian-American historian has written that if he used the methods of computation of German and Scottish-Irish historians, he could "prove" that there were many thousands of Italians in the American Revolutionary armies. As if to show his own susceptibility, that same historian remarks elsewhere, "The proportion of Italian officers and enlisted men who served during the Civil War was perhaps the highest of any ethnic group."[2]

The flyer announcing a 1981 conference in Washington, sponsored by the National Italian American Foundation, gives the following quotation from a well-known Italian-American educator:

> The Italians have been the most important ethnic group in their influence on the creation of America. This influence starts as early as the fifteenth century

> and extends well into the nineteenth century. It is only during the seventeenth and eighteenth centuries that other ethnic groups because of their larger numbers in America begin to influence the mores and habits of the white man as he populates our continent.[3]

A short litany of the way men of culture have taken "their stand in history" causes embarrassment. Was Peter Francesco, the giant foundling who saved George Washington's life, Italian or Portuguese? Were the glassblowers who carried out the first strike for labour justice at Jamestown in the 1600s, Poles or Venetians? Did Columbus discover America, or was he a johnny-come-lately after the Vikings or St. Brendan in a leather or stone boat? And how would the resolution of these disputes enhance or diminish the status of the Italian ethnic group in North America? Can Italian Canada avoid these games which a misreading of multicultural policy in relation to ethnic studies seems to encourage?

I wish here to prejudge neither the validity of the retrospective discovery of some early Italian-Canadian heroes nor the significance of those heroes' ethnicity in their own time. For although as a trained psychiatrist, Fanon would have recognized the near hysterical uses of history in that Italian-American educator's claim, he also understood and sympathized with the need for this "passionate research and this anger," which are important to the individual in the "sphere of psycho-effective equilibrium." As a good Marxist he nonetheless saw such nationalist and ethnocentric use of history as dangerous, as a form of false consciousness. "I am ready to concede," he wrote in *The Wretched of the Earth*,

> that on the plane of factual being the past existence of an Aztec civilization does not change anything very much in the diet of the Mexican peasant of today. I admit that also proofs of a wonderful Songhai civilization will not change the fact that today the Songhais are underfed and illiterate, thrown between sky and water with empty heads and empty eyes.

There is a risk in using claims of a "glorious past" as a tactic to combat bigotry. Such usage implies that contemporaneous unglossed reality somehow provides the bigoted with a legitimate case and assumes that when a people's "glorious past" is made known, bigotry withers away. Fanon observed that the native and, we might add, some ethnic intellectuals have the secret hope of "discovering beyond the misery of today, beyond self-contempt, resignation and abjuration some very beautiful and splendid era whose existence rehabilitates us both in regard to ourselves and in regard to others."[4] For much of Italian America's ethnic intelligentsia, this means emphasis on a golden age before 1850, an era when the only Italian Americans were artists and sculptors; when a Tuscan named Mazzei was explaining democracy to Thomas Jefferson; when the adjective "Italian" evoked images of Mozart's librettist, Lorenzo DaPonte, who was in New York to establish the opera; of Cesnola who founded the Metropolitan Museum of Art; of Garibaldi and other *profughi* (political refugees), heirs to ancient democratic and republican traditions, finding refuge in the nation born of those antique dreams.

For the Italian-Canadian intelligentsia, status comes from finding Italians a place as an auxiliary founding people. The need to achieve "psycho-effective equilibrium," has led to what I call *scopritorismo* — a hunt for the *Italianità* of warriors, priests and explorers of Italian descent serving New France. Thus, names like General Bourlamacque and De Ligne become Burlamacchi and De Lino; Henri de Tonty must be recorded as Enrico Di Tonti and Father Bressan as Bressani or Bresciani.[5] No one tries to ascertain the sense of identity or the sentiments of those heroes, some of whom were Italian-born and Italian in culture, while others merely had ancestors from the Italian peninsula.

In the United States, and increasingly in Canada, the urge to own a respectable North American pedigree leads the various ethnic intelligentsia into the vapid and vacuous struggle to get the face of Filippo Mazzei or Giovanni Caboto on a postage stamp, reminiscent of the campaigns of Mussolini's consuls in the 1930s to *italianizzare* the *colonie* by rallying the innocent population around the effort to have Cabot declared the official discoverer of Canada.

Another symptom of the need for a glorious past is the increase of small conferences dedicated to pioneering Italians, most especially those that satisfy the urge for respectability — sculptors, artists, musical *maestri*, scholars, *profughi* and noblemen. Such conferences often seem more intent on asserting how different these immigrants were from the later *poveri miserabili*, than on explaining the continuing causes and processes of immigration. Whatever the scholarly value of such gatherings, they have a complexly negative relationship to the history and perception of the post-1885 mass immigration of Italians to North America. Asked about that later "mean" and "bas-Italian" migration, organizers and participants tend to become sullen; they are uncomfortable when one talks about more common folk, immigrants who were *suonatori ambulanti* (street musicians and hurdy-gurdy men), *figuristi* and *chincaglieri* (casters of cheap statuary and pedlars) and, worse yet, *contadini* (unskilled peasants turned ditch diggers in North America).

The discomfort with the "other" history, the "mean history of our people" as it was labelled at one conference, which seems to surround the simultaneous assertion of roots and bourgeois respectability, suggests that Italian North Americans suffer from a condition which the ancient Greeks called *atimia*. Here we can translate *atimia* as ethnic self-disesteem, a phenomenon observed unsympathetically by a scholar writing in the *American Journal of Sociology* during the Second World War. He seems to have understood the way in which *atimia*, an ethnic inferiority complex, led to aggressive, ethnocentric assertions and to recitals of the ethnic group's past glories that in fact flirted with racism. He wrote:

> Italian ethnocentricism on the other hand is centered about the accomplishments of the inhabitants of Italy during the last two thousands years. On the assumption that any great man produced at any time during this period is proof enough that all individuals born within the group have all the biological potentialities of genius. "There is no nationality that produced more great people than the Italians. The Italians have contributed more to civilization than many other people. The greatest painters, sculptors, writers and composers have been Italian." This postulate should, however, be taken as defense against the helplessness in which Italians find themselves both in Europe and the United States.[6]

By invoking the greatness that was or is Italy, that was or is Italian culture, by parading the special skills of the early immigrant elites, the Italian North American intelligentsia is in danger of allowing the ethno-psychiatric uses of history — the skewing of perception that filio-pietism combined with *atimia* causes — to usurp serious study of the processes of Italian migration. Such celebrations provide a surrogate history, one that avoids coming to terms with the real history which requires accepting the humbler human dignity of Italians who came during the mass migration after 1885. That denial of history, that misdirection of research energy, of ethnic pride and, increasingly, of funding contributes to a failure to appreciate the heroism and human resourcefulness of the eight million Italian migrants who helped civilize the Americas.

The *atimia* which provokes this response is especially sad because at its source is a misconception born in the nineteenth century and fostered by the political intelligentsia in Italy, by the consular service, and by Italian travellers to North America's Little Italies. Much of that Italian national intelligentsia had a psychological problem of its own: unity of the peninsula had not brought great power status, had not brought true imperial status, but rather humiliating defeat at the hands of Ethiopia. The result was a national inferiority complex among Italian intellectuals and officials which fostered irredentism, fascism and an image of emigration as haemorrhage.[7] Italian consular officials, usually recruited from the urban upper classes and often from the North, shared this sense of national embarrassment and thus misinterpreted Anglo-Saxon prejudice. The consuls believed that the first cause of prejudice was the Italian migrants themselves (*girovaghi*) and the large numbers of *suonatori ambulanti*, "che sono i peggiori e più inutili della specie" (who are the worst and most useless of the race).[8]

This view of the immigrants as *cafoni* from whom one had to distance oneself was shared by almost all those political intelligentsia, consuls, clergy and, then later, *fuorusciti* (political exiles), who made opinion and shaped the image by which immigrants measured their worth. Distance from the "mean history" of the Little Italy could be maintained by emphasizing blood ties to the glories that were Italian culture or by claiming to be from among the earlier immigrants, or well-born, or skilled, or simply northern. People who need to assert their superiority to the general migrant stream exist, of course, in every immigrant cohort and are best caricatured by the joke that emerged from the Hungarian Revolution of 1956. In that story two dachshunds are crossing the Hungarian border into Austria to escape the Soviet repression. As they cross the border, one turns to the other and says, "I don't know about you, but in the old country my parents were German shepherds." Studying those explorers, priests and soldiers of Italian descent who participated in early Canadian history then becomes more than an exercise in filio-pietist chronicling; it is a search for symbolic German shepherds. Since it goes on in the psychologically and competitively charged atmosphere of our "multicultural" times, it acquires political significance.

A pantheon of Italian-Canadian heroes, rediscovered from the recesses of the earlier accounts, is being refurbished for contemporaneous needs. At the apex is the discoverer of Canada, Giovanni Caboto, a.k.a. John Cabot. Other figures are Father Francesco Bressani, the Jesuit missionary who wrote his *Breve Relazione* on Canada's Indians in Italian, though only a French translation was known in

Canada for many years. The majority of the pantheon is made up of soldiers and adventurers serving the French Regime such as Enrico di Tonti, De La Salle's second in command, the Crisafi brothers, the Marini brothers and François-Charles Bourlamacque (Bourlamacque's grandfather, Burlamacchi, had migrated from Italy to France), third in command to Montcalm.[9]

North America's historical myths and political paradigms about the founding of nations took little notice of those who did not belong to the dominant political or ethnic groups and so the role of these individuals has been generally discounted or subsumed into the myths of the regnant culture. Perhaps the best Canadian instance of this was the tendency to portray the discoverer Caboto as a Bristol English gentleman named Cabot rather than to explain his Venetian and Genoese family heritage. Of course, Italian-Canadian responses to that slight — the insistence that Cabot be seen as Giovanni Caboto, an Italian — has, on occasion, been equally manipulative of history. Between the hegemonic filio-pietists of the "Old Stock" and those who challenge them, there is little difference of view about the right to mould historical evidence for the needs of the political culture.

Caboto's family history was typical of that shaped by the chaotic petty state system of the disunited Italian peninsula. Italian seafarers, merchants and soldiers took to foreign service and were at the vanguard of Spanish, Portuguese, English and French exploration of the Western Hemisphere. In no instance could they carry on their trade or their explorations for an Italian State. The career and sentiments of Caboto's father reflected his times. He is said to have given up his Genoese citizenship for the Venetian one because of the "prospettiva d'un migliore avvenire'' — the prospect of a better future — for himself and his children. Remarkably that very phrase ''prospettiva d'un migliore avvenire'' often appears, more than four centuries later, in the reports of prefects throughout Italy, which try to explain why, beyond *la miseria* and seductive steamship recruiting *agenti*, the common people emigrated in vast numbers.

Caboto's motive probably differed little from those of the millions of labourers and peasants who came to North America in the nineteenth and twentieth centuries, men whose philosophy of survival, like Caboto's, was summed up in the Latin proverb, *Ubi panis, ibi patria*. Despite his symbolic importance to the Italian-Canadian search for a place in the history of the founding peoples in Canada, serious study of Giovanni Caboto has not advanced or been very central in Canadian scholarship. There are occasional Italian-Canadian works of filio-piety, but certainly we know more of Cabot from American and British maritime historians like Morrison and Williamson than from any equivalent Canadian source.[10] The grievance expressed by elements of the Italian-Canadian intelligentsia that Cabot is little studied and little understood in Canada then deserves a hearing, although the omission is less glaring when placed in the context of scholarly neglect of fifteenth and sixteenth-century Canada generally.

Most of the facts of Cabot's public life and career are not subject to much dispute. However, ascribing to him in some simple form sentiments of either ''Englishness'' or ''Italianness'' is not very useful. Like many men of his time, Cabot possessed multiple and shifting loyalties. His ethnocultural sense of self, if a man of that century can be said to have had one, may have been a continuum, or various loyalties may have superseded and conflicted with one another over time. Indeed, he may have seen all ethnic or national loyalties simply as flags of convenience for the Caboto family. In other words, he may have, in the modern phrase, "negotiated his ethnicity" continuously, according to circumstance and encounter. In a continuum of possible loyalties, where did the Anglicized adventurer John Cabot, the Italian Giovanni Caboto and the naturalized Venetian Zuan Cabot stand? Was his first loyalty to his Genoese birthplace, his Venetian family and business connections, his Italian culture, his Catholic cosmopolitanism, the Bristol business community, or the English king who employed him?

Giovanni Caboto, when he landed in Cape Breton in 1497, planted a cross and two flags — the Royal Standard of England and the banner of St. Mark, the patron of the Venetian city state that had been his second home. There was, of course, no Italian *tricolore* yet created for him to plant. Would he have planted the *tricolore* if it had existed? The bare facts of Caboto's career cannot tell the reader with any certainty about the explorer's Italianity or lack of it.

It would be wise to pause and make a general comment on the anachronism of applying concepts of ethnicity to the early modern period. I do so not to dim the colours of the emerging Italian oriflammes in the pantheon of Canada's founding peoples, but to remind us of what our thought processes are when we try to assess the numerical importance of an ethnic group in the North American past. The question of the meaning of what we call, in modern terms, ethnic identity is vexed. And we are unlikely to capture the true sense of self-identity, or of hierarchies of sentiments and loyalties, which a man harboured centuries ago simply by equating his surname with some modern nationality or his ethnic sentiment with his place of origin. Such exercises in ethnic labelling are best left to the Canadian census-takers. Because of the nationalist inculcation we have received in Canadian and Italian schools, it is difficult to grasp the cosmopolitanism and easy multilingualism which prevailed among the upper classes of the Italian peninsula until after the French Revolution. This way of being and its style may be epitomized by the great Habsburg soldier of the eighteenth century who signed himself Eugenio von Savoie, that is trilingually. Was he an Austrian, a Piedmontese , a Frenchman? Did he feel himself Italian or German? Caboto himself signed his name differently in different phases of his life. Would these questions about identity make sense to him, and, if not, is it sensible for the modern historian to ask them?

However damaging to historical truth and fraught with structural prejudice is the Canadian habit of Anglicizing or Gallicizing the names and, by extension, the realities of men like Caboto, Tonti and Bressani, the practice of applying high levels of Italianity to them leads to further pitfalls. It tends to underestimate their cosmopolitan fealty to their social class and European Christendom, or simply Catholicism. It assumes that loyalty to city and family were in continuum with the post-Napoleonic sense of nationality and feelings of patriotism for the nation-state. Mazzini, of course, knew better and recognized that the "insurrection," which was the Risorgimento, would have to be followed by the "revolution," which in his mind would be the establishment of a national school system educating Italians to their shared culture and destiny. Gramsci has commented precisely and acidly on this need of the Italian "hegemonic liberal bourgeoisie" to encourage the common people in a cult of past national accomplishments in the fields of exploration and warfare in order to draw attention away from the contemporaneous squalour and powerlessness of post-Risorgimento Italy. I do not claim here that North American ethnic leadership is so clever, evil, or successfully hegemonic.[11]

It is incumbent on scholarship, especially that imbued with a humane passion for telling the story correctly, to prove the *italianità* of those Italian Canadians emerging in the pantheon of Canada's founding greats. If scholars can do so in a thoughtful and researched way, then learning will be served and the governing narratives, or what Foucault calls "reigns of truth," of the two founding peoples at least will be brought into question in a manner which might be beneficial for contemporaneous intergroup relations. This work cannot therefore be done as filio-pietistically as that of the earlier anglophone and French historians: all immigrants know they must be better to be as good as the "Old Stock." The upbringing, language-use, mores, folkways and environmental experience, the "ethnoversion" of Caboto and Bressani, need to be subjects of scholarship not speculation. Otherwise we come dangerously close to suggesting that what is significant, what links the Cabotos and Bressanis to modern Italian Canadians, is some concept of shared Italian "blood." Indeed, Father Vangelisti made such a link by describing early Italian-Canadian heroes as people of whom Italians could be proud and who reflected "una limpida e tersa luce sul nostro sangue..." (a limpid and clear light on our blood).[12]

That noun, blood, despite its allegorical charm, refers to a genetic pool. Its unsophisticated use in our search for the "Adams" of each ethnic group in Canada is not harmless; it accustoms us to think in biological, somatic and racial terms about ethnic history and contemporary ethnicity. Italian-Canadian heritage-boosters should not flirt with such imagery, even if Anglo-Canadian historians only very recently, if at all, have given up the apparently allegorical uses of the word "race" to explain historical behaviour. Donald Creighton praised the stoicism "so characteristic of (Prime Minister Wilfrid) Laurier's race," and John Dafoe could describe Laurier's mind as "typically French with something else Italianate about it, an inheritance from the long-dead Savoyard ancestors who brought the name to this continent."[13] The hunt for Italianity of blood in New France becomes more comprehensible in this context of the use of such racialist language in mainstream Canadian historical writing. But it is no less reprehensible, if only because such abuses have brought exclusion or discrimination in North America upon the parents and grandparents of those who now play historical bloodhounds.

In the late 1920s, shortly before the 400th anniversary of Jacques Cartier's reconnaissance of the Canadian coast (1534) and in the face of some virulently hostile French-Canadian opinion, the Montreal newspaper *Il Cittadino* began to agitate for the official recognition of Cabot as discoverer of Canada (*scopritore del Canada*). This campaign was encouraged by the Italian fascist consul in Montreal and taken up by *notabili* in various Canadian cities: Toronto, North Bay and Hamilton, among others. Since 1897 a plaque had been in place in the Nova Scotia legislature to commemorate the 400th anniversary of Cabot's landing. Now, in the wake of the *Cittadino*'s agitation, funds were raised for a Caboto memorial in Montreal. But in order to salve French-Canadian sensibilities about Cartier, the community thought it wise to put off the planned ceremonies to honour the *scopritore*.[14] Eventually, a statue of Caboto was presented to Mayor Camillien Houde by the so-called doyen of the community, Onorato (Honoré) Catelli, and it was duly put in place opposite the Forum. Subsequently, the name of Caboto was increasingly used by Italian Canadians for their clubs and halls. Even though the *Cittadino*'s campaign took place under suspect auspices and was a device by the fascist consular service to rally Italian Canadians behind Mussolini's nationalism in the world, it was supported energetically by most Italian Canadians.

Mussolini, of course, encouraged them from the start. In a letter responding to an invitation from the Montreal committee to honour Caboto, he struck an insightful note about the ties that bound Caboto to the modern Italian immigrants:

> Giovanni Caboto, whose name you wish to honour as that of the man who discovered the land where today you live as welcome and hardworking *ospiti* [guests] is a symbol of the *genialità* and of the daring with which our great Fathers then, and our tenacious brothers now, have brought their labour and vibrancy to new lands.

But the *Duce* also stated that his Italy joined in honouring Caboto, not least because it was "seeking to reaffirm her ancient greatness upon the seas."

Mackenzie King, for his part, also touched on the proper themes of integration into Canadian life and praise of those talents of virtuosity which he presumably assumed all Italians shared:

> It is a great honour for the Italians to be associated in such a direct manner with events which signal the beginning of the new age and it is typical since men of their race have always stood at the forefront in all spheres of human activity, in that of the intellect, of the imagination, of science and of art. The names of Galileo, Dante, Michelangelo, to mention only a few, prove that assertion.[15]

Many organizers of Caboto committees found themselves, like the Sons of Italy, compromised by their ties, innocent or purposeful, with *consolar-fascismo* when World War II broke out. Still the annual Caboto celebrations in Montreal on June 24 survived, and in 1955 the Montreal square containing the statue was renamed Caboto Square. Mr. Pickersgill, the Minister of Citizenship and Immigration was present and the ceremony represented a political echo of the new Italian mass migration to Canada then underway. But until the emergence of multicultural policy in the 1970s and the renewed ethnic steeplechase to be ''assistant Canadians,'' public interest in Caboto as *scopritore* declined. In fact, efforts to use Columbus as an emblematic figure eclipsed the Caboto lobby between 1945 and 1975.

In the 1970s new Italian-Canadian spokesmen showed concern for what they believed to be the lack of just recognition both of Caboto's role as discoverer of Canada and Caboto's essential Italianness. They saw the use of the English surname, Cabot, as both cause and effect of this neglect. The two issues, while apparently separate, tended to come together. One Toronto Italian magazine, *Comunità Viva*, has dedicated much space in various issues over the decade to the drive for the *riconoscimento dello scopri-*

tore del Canada. Senator Peter Bosa recommended in a December 6, 1979 speech to the Senate that the government remedy the improper Anglicization of Caboto's name in Canadian toponymy so that, for example, the Cabot Trail would become the Caboto Trail.

It is worth trying to understand Senator Bosa's reasoning.[16] First, he believed that there was no evidence that Caboto ever wished to be known by any name other than Giovanni Caboto. Then he explained his understanding of the civic uses of history to the chamber:

> The fact of knowing that our predecessors have had a significant role in the discovery of this nation inculcates in us a sense of pride. There are many other personages among us who have made their contribution in diverse ways and in diverse times in the history of Canada. Some of these are: the navigator and explorer Giovanni Da Verrazano in 1524, the assistant to De La Salle, Enrico Tonti in 1678, the governor of Trois-Rivières, Captain Crisafi in 1703, Brigadier-General Carlo Burlamacchi, third in command to General Montcalm, Joseph Marini, a senior officer who was killed in the Battle of the Plains of Abraham in 1759.

Senator Bosa's efforts to give Caboto back his Italianity irked some Anglo-Canadians. The narrow-mindedness of some of the public responses to this gave him an opportunity to expand on his reasons for emphasizing the Italian role in early Canadian history. Those reasons are worth repeating at length since the Senator's views reflect an era in which the official policy of multiculturalism encourages concepts such as ethnic heritage, "contribution" and group longevity on the Canadian scene.

First, the Senator considered it important to celebrate pluralism of origin as a way of enforcing an egalitarian, open-minded and shared sense of Canadian history:

> However the most valid reason for recognizing people of various ethnic backgrounds who have played a part in the history of Canada is that it instills in the people from those ethnic groups a sense of pride, a feeling of belonging and more important still a feeling of being part of this country.
>
> These feelings and emotions are the very essence that gives Canadians a common denominator which binds them to one another. History shows that loyalty to a country and national unity are more prevalent in a nation where its citizens have something in common with their past and share a common goal for the present and the future.
>
> I endeavour to promote this concept which is a concept that is not always understood and I hope that other Canadians who realize how important it is to strengthen national unity in this area will take the lead in encouraging recognition of legitimate contribution made to Canada's history by anyone, regardless of his or her ethnic background.[17]

For much the same reasons, the Senator, along with people like the editor of *Comunità Viva*, favour the use of Caboto as an emblematic name for Italian-Canadian organizations, buildings and projects. The use of Columbus (as in Columbus Centre and Villa Colombo) has acquired an insidiously continentalist resonance from an American tradition in which the explorer became a symbol to unite Italian Americans. The Columbian tradition is seen as less relevant to Italian Canadians or as positively subversive of some potential Canadian civic identity.[18]

More problematic is the other declared reason for emphasizing the early Italian contribution to Canada, a reason which seems to reflect both *atimia* and a tendency to see history as a therapeutic tool for contemporary interethnic relations and, thus, something that is adjusted for a civic good. Responding to criticism of his desire to reassert Cabot's Italianity by changing place names, the Senator wrote:

> Most of the news relating to people with Italian names is invariably negative to the point that Canadians have a distorted image of Canadians of Italian origin. In support of this view I am enclosing a survey on public opinion, as well as a press release dated July 13, 1979. I believe that as a parliamentarian, it is my duty to correct the false image that Canadian society has of a large segment of Canadian citizens. My view is shared by my parliamentary colleagues, the Human Rights Commissioner, as well as prominent members of the law enforcement agencies. I am sure that every Canadian who is free from racial prejudice will see the English fair play in this objective. What possible injurious consequences could be derived from restoring a name to its original spelling?[19]

What injury indeed; although one can understand that changing the name of a trail from Cabot to Caboto undoes for many people a century of local history and usage. Nor does a campaign to identify heroes of an

Italian-Canadian past seem a very effective weapon against defamation of Italians by the North American media. It is unlikely that a documentary on Caboto would appeal to the CBC as much as the market possibilities of a series, such as "Connections," which trades cheaply on the "mafia mystique." However, the reader by this point can hardly deny that study of the Italian-Canadian pantheon of explorers, priests and soldiers is an aspect of contemporary multicultural politics. The attempt to have a Caboto Day declared a Canadian holiday would bring both current rhetoric and the malleability of the past to its highest pitch. But a glance at the history of the struggle to make Columbus Day a national rather than a state option holiday in the United States should daunt the organizers.

The imminence of Caboto's meaning for Canadian history and for Italian Canadians; the ambiguity about race, sovereignty, identity, ethnicity, involved in invoking his name today, can be glimpsed in the words of Guglielmo Vangelisti, a Servite priest in Montreal, who ranks as the best amateur historian of the Italians in Canada to date. In 1958 he wrote that in Caboto we remember "the great Italian who *gave* England her right on the continent, a right which the colonizing spirit of his sons profits from much later on."[20] The good father's theme is reminiscent of Crispi's parliamentary address on Empire delivered in 1888: "Gentlemen, Italy arrived far too late in the family of great powers. She had the honour of discovering America but did not have the strength to impose her dominion there..."[21]

Thus as early as the 1950s, Father Vangelisti seemed to be claiming first place for Italy among the contributors to the making of Canada. Part of the vehemence which surrounds this discussion may have to do with the fact that in the filio-pietist steeplechase for first place, Cabot served as the British entry against Cartier many years before the Italians seized his colours. Vangelisti seems to have shared this simple faith that the "old stock would stop resting on their priority in the land" and recognize their non-British, non-French neighbours as peers in Canadian history and society.[22]

"The roles of the French and British communities have dominated the written history of Canada. Contributions by Canadians of other cultural origins have received little attention. As a result most history books present an incomplete record of Canada's past." These words in a government hand-out called *Multicultural Update* (October 1978) seem to promise, or threaten, instant redress and a reworking of the textbooks. They remind us too that as the justification or basis for hegemony changes, the "caretakers" of the nation see the rewriting of history as a tool for fashioning contemporary society. No doubt, for those uneasy with the concept of "contribution" and unhappy with the apparent attempt to push aside the charter groups to make room for others, such assertions by the Multiculturalism Directorate of the federal Department of the Secretary of State might be reminiscent of the efforts made in the 1920s by the Chicago School Board. Under the influence of German and Irish-American politicians, the Board tried to create a new history of the American Revolution for schoolchildren which "must not be pro-British statistically or psychologically." As one wag wrote then:

Every people and race
In Chicago will trace
Its hand in the ousting of Britain
We shall learn 'twas our town

That pulled George the III down
When the real revolution is written[23]

It is within this atmosphere where the record of the past is malleable and is made to serve the civic good or the therapeutic needs of those uneasy about their status in the land, that most writing about Canada's ethnic past now goes on. Ethnic studies within multicultural policy should not be reduced to that same sort of ancestor-worship, to that same sort of confusion of individual pyschological well-being with that of the Canadian nation-state as now lurks in the Canadian nationalist historiographical mainstream. Even if we are on the edge of a post-nationalist age and a global village, however, it is not likely that many immigrant groups will have the courage and dignity to reject such manufactured national traditions, especially if these are slightly amended to include them. The consequence will be: 1. an emphasis on a history of warriors, priests, notables and artists at the expense of the other heritage, which is of immigrant families and the more immediate history of their peasant, artisan and labourer parents and grandparents; 2. a search for instances of what Redfield has called the "great tradition" at the expense of the "little tradition" of common people; and 3. an avoidance of the study of issues of capitalist exploitation, segmented work-forces and the accompanying justificatory super-structure of prejudice toward migrants and ethnics.

Like his father and those who came later from Italy, Caboto lived within a pattern of the flow of labour to capital, talent to opportunity, a pattern in which national boundaries counted for little. Perhaps he and they would understand the dangers inherent in the retrospective distortion which turns immigrant history into the history of nation-states and notables.

NOTES

1. Frantz Fanon, *The Wretched of the Earth* (New York, 1968), 209.

2. G. Schiavo, *The Italians in America before the Civil War* (New York, 1934), 266, 279.

3. P. Sammartino cited on jacket in Andre Rolle, *The Italian Americans: Troubled Roots* (New York, 1980). For a critique of the Canadian situation see R.F. Harney, "Entwined Fortunes: Multiculturalism and Ethnic Studies in Canada," in *Siirtolaisuus-Migration* 3 (Turku, Finland, 1984).

4. Fanon, *Wretched of the Earth*, 209-11.

5. Guglielmo Vangelisti, *Gli Italiani in Canada*, 2nd ed. (Montreal, 1958), remains the most thorough genealogical and historical study of early Italians in Canada. Recently the Library of Parliament, Research Branch, has prepared historical reports on a number of early Canadians of Italian descent for Senator Peter Bosa. The latter has kindly made these available to me. The reports carry the curious caveat that such projects "are designed in accordance with the requirements and instructions of the Member making the request. The views expressed should not therefore be regarded as those of the Research Branch..."

6. D. Rodnick, "Group Frustration in Connecticut," *American Journal of Sociology* XLVI, 2 (Sept. 1941), 159-60. Such a view of "blood" in history is obviously not an ethnic malady alone. Behind much local history and genealogical study, the same urge to use "longevity in the land" or illustrious ancestors to bolster newfound respectability operates. One might even see its traces in the determinedly national frame of post-colonial Canadian historiography.

7. See, for examples of *atimia* among Italian diplomats, the various consular responses in L. Carpi, *Delle Colonie e dell'emigrazione italiana all'estero sotto l'aspetto dell'industria, commercio e agricoltura e con trattazioni d'importanti questioni sociali* (Milano, 1874) II, 80-145. See also, L. Villari, "L'Opinione pubblica americana e i nostri emigrati," *Nuova Antologia* CCXXXII (1910), 503. For a general discussion of the issue, see A. Aquarone, "The Impact of Emigration on Italian Public Opinion and Politics," in *The United States and Italy: the First Two Hundred Years*, Acts of the American Italian Historical Association, H. Nelli, ed. (Washington, 1976). The campaign to create a Marconi museum in Cape Breton, led by a recent Italian ambassador, displayed some of the same tendency to ignore the "mean" history for the "glorious." Glace Bay and Dominion, where Marconi lived for a few years, have been home to Trevisan coal-miners since before the turn of the century; Calabrians and others helped build Whitney Pier in Sydney shortly after 1900. None of their story, apparently, seemed important to the museum's organizers.

8. R. Paulucci de Calboli, *Girovaghi italiani in Inghilterra ed i suonatori ambulanti* (Città di Castello, 1898), 5.

9. Vangelisti, *Gli Italiani* used in conjunction with L. Le Jeune's *Dictionnaire général de biographie, histoire, littérature, agriculture, commerce industrie et des arts, sciences, mœurs, institutions politiques et religieuses du Canada* (Ottawa, n.d.) remains

the quickest way to discover something about these early Italians, more specifically whether they were Italian-born or from families long removed from the peninsula. Some confusion results from the fact that the Vangelisti volume, published in Italian, presents Italian forms of most surnames; Le Jeune naturally presents French spellings. The first filio-pietist use of these Italians, it is important to note, seems to have come, not from within the group, but from J.M. Gibbon whose proto-multicultural patriotic volume of 1937, *The Canadian Mosaic: the Making of a Northern Nation*, actually suggested that General Bourlamacque, Montcalm's aide, was born in Italy. Le Jeune and Vangelisti describe Bourlamacque as a Parisian noble with an Italian grandfather. C.P. Stacey, in the *Dictionary of Canadian Biography*, remarked that "Bourlamaque is said to have been of Italian descent." In the 1970s the Research Branch of the Library of Parliament, undoubtedly sensing the multicultural temper of the times, wrote, "It is often forgotten that an Italian F.C. Burlamacchi, called Bourlamaque in French, served as Montcalm's third in command." Obviously, one's ethnicity in North America continues to be a matter of negotiation even beyond the grave.

10. I have depended on the following for details about Caboto: J.A. Williamson, *The Cabot Voyage and Bristol Discovery under Henry VII* (Cambridge, 1972); S.E. Morrison, *The European Discovery of America. The Northern Voyages* (Oxford, 1971); S.E. Dawson, *The Voyages of the Cabots. Transactions of the Royal Society of Canada* III, 2 (1897).

11. A. Gramsci, *Gli Intelletuali e l'organizzazione della cultura* (Rome, 1971), 78-80.

12. Vangelisti, *Gli Italiani*, 70.

13. J. Levitt, "Race and Nation in Canadian Anglophone Historiography," *Canadian Review of Studies in Nationalism* VIII, 1 (Spring 1981), 1-16.

14. Roberto Perin, "Conflits d'identité et d'allégeance. La propagande du consulat italien à Montréal dans les années 1930," *Questions de Culture No 2: Migrations et Communautés Culturelles* (Ottawa, 1982), 81-102. See, for example, *Il Cittadino of Montreal* editorial of 26 September 1934, which observes "... the French Canadian press dauntlessly carries on its campaign to the detriment of the glory appertaining to one of our race."

15. Mussolini's and Mackenzie King's letters appear in "In onore di Giovanni Caboto," *Bollettino dell'Emigrazione*, no. 7 (Rome, 1927), 1007-09.

16. I would like to thank Senator Bosa for providing me with copies of his speeches about Caboto, of letters received in response to those speeches and research work done for him by the Library of Parliament. If this paper seems critical of his views of history and skeptical about his belief that improved knowledge of an Italian-Canadian past can combat Italophobia now, I wish to record here my respect for his energy, commitment and ceaseless work on behalf of the Italian-Canadian community.

17. Senator Peter Bosa, Speech to the Senate, 6 December 1979.

18. "Occasioni perdute," in *Comunità Viva* IX, 6-7 (June 1980), p. 34. Other issues of *Comunità Viva* with extensive sections on the issue of Caboto as *scopritore* appeared in September 1972, April 1975, May 1978. In a letter to the editor in 1972, a reader expressed the relationship among Canadianism, multiculturalism and *italianità*

well, "I see that our neighbours honor Colombo, even though they call him Columbus, why shouldn't we honor Giovanni Caboto who had the merit of discovering Canada, this marvellous land that has also given us Multiculturalism in order to 'sentire affratellati e sullo stesso piano civico.'"

19. Letter of Senator Bosa to former constituent, 22 January 1980.

20. Vangelisti, *Gli Italiani*, 20: "il grande italiano, che diede all'Inghilterra un diritto sul continente, che lo spirito colonizzatore dei suoi figli mise a profitto più tardi."

21. Francesco Crispi, *Discorsi parlamentari* (Rome, 1915), Vol. 3, 75-76.

22. R.F. Harney, "*E Pluribus Unum*: Louis Adamic and the Meaning of Ethnic History," *Journal of Ethnic Studies* 14,1 (Spring 1986).

23. E.R. Lewis, *America. Nation or Confusion: a Study of Our Immigration Problems* (New York, 1928), 342.

Italian Emigration: Reconsidering the Links in Chain Migration

Franc Sturino

Chain Migration and the Question of Scale

In the study of Italian migration to the New World, chain migration has been one of the most fruitful concepts used to throw light on the dynamics of the movement. Although the image of a chain-like movement linking places of origin with specific destinations can be found on both sides of the Atlantic in the literature contemporaneous with the era of mass migration at the turn of the century,[1] it was not until after World War II that a systematic study of migration chains emerged. It was primarily the research conducted by Australian scholars anxious to understand the post-war — and heavily Southern European — influx into their country that raised chain migration from an image to an influential analytical tool.[2]

Within this "Canberra School" of historical demography the work of John S. Macdonald has been foremost in building a theory of chain migration.[3] In contrast to simple economic models of labour migration and to State concentration on impersonally organized movement, Macdonald drew attention to social and informal forces determining Italian migration. It is worth quoting his now classic definition:

> Chain migration can be defined as that movement in which prospective migrants learn of opportunities, are provided with transportation, and have initial accommodation and employment arranged *by means of primary social relationships with previous migrants.*[4]

Macdonald distinguishes three basically sequential types of chains for the period between 1880 and World War I: the migration of males through labour agents or *padroni*; the serial migration of workers through the assistance of other established lone labourers; delayed family migration uniting wives and children with breadwinners.

This conceptualization has withstood the test of time and has influenced many students of immigration. Especially in the Italian case, chain migration theory has proven to be compelling for a number of reasons. First, it provides an elegant model which explains the selectivity in Italian migration. Rather than being drawn evenly from throughout the peninsula Italian immigrants were quite narrowly drawn from particular locations, and were quite precisely directed to a specific, limited number of New World destinations. Second, the theory goes a long way to explain how the "latent functions of informal networks," by and large triumphed over the "manifest functions of State bureaucracies." In other words, it explains how the aim of peasant-based emigrants of entering New World countries proved successful over governments which sought their restriction, if not exclusion, on the basis of some measure of undesirability, at root racialist, even when couched in cultural and economic terms. Third, focusing on the New World side of the relation, chain migration theory helps to explain patterns of settlement. The workings of early padronism, the typology of immigrant residential concentrations, the development of occupational and industrial niches, and similar themes have become interwoven with chain migration theory.

While it is clear that all this has contributed much to the study of Italian migration, and while some notable work has recently been done to refine the concept, one important lacuna remains.[5] Little systematic investigation has taken place to determine the "shape" of the migration chains, that is the parameters within which chains actually operated. In this regard the chain concept remains more hieroglyphic than analytic. The question of scale has simply not received sustained examination. Yet, this would seem to be a priority since a clear definition of the "narrowness" or "broadness" of chains is important for understanding many central issues ranging from the dynamics of chain destination and diversion to the nature of immigrant insertion into the host society.

This is not to say that there is no mention of scale in the literature on immigration. On the contrary, studies on Italian migration are full of references to village, district and provincial chains, indeed chains at almost all possible levels of association ranging from family to *regione*.[6] And this is precisely the problem. How can such variation emerge in a field of study in which one would assume there are basic points of agreement? It could be argued that different levels of linkage are not mutually exclusive, that they can co-exist depending on specific variables (the sheer size of grouping by common origin being the most obvious). But there has been no attempt to delineate what these variables are, let alone analyze the conditions under which one or another, predominate. Moreover, even if various levels of linkage existed, the question remains as to which level had primacy, was most representative, most functional in forging and driving the chain. The following discussion deals with this question of scale.

Local Area and Social Space

Migration chains are activated by "primary social relationships." This means of course that people must know each other at a more or less personal level; they must be bound together in some concrete way so as to make use of relationships in the migration process. It seems logical that knowing the socio-economic parameters of the potential emigrants' lives in the Old World would help in determining the scale of migration chains.

Parameters of intercourse have geographic boundaries. Two main territorially bound migration chains are referred to in the literature: provincial (or district) and village chains. The province is generally too wide a unit for migration chains to operate, since at this level people become anonymous and hence personal contacts could not be used to generate movement in the chain. The "village" has been more appropriate as a unit of analysis. However, it has been influenced by the anthropological notion of *campanilismo*.[7] "Village-mindedness" supposedly pervaded rural Italy and the experiences and world view of the inhabitants were largely "confined within the shadow cast by [the] town campanile."[8] In contrast to this, recent work in social history illustrates that the reality of peasant life involved contacts well beyond the village.[9] Furthermore, the limits of the village were simply too narrow to supply all of the emigrants' needs to their best advantage; for example, finding favourable loans, literate intermediaries, or appropriate New World contacts.

Emphasis on the province and rural municipality have the advantage that as juridical and political units both their emigrations can be conveniently researched through the consultation of public records. Such a focus can overlook intermediate units of association, within which personal contacts were possible and more suited to the migration process. It was to such a unit of interpersonal contact, intermediate between the village and *provincia*, that my own research led.

Originally, in a project involving a case study of chain migration from Southern Italy to North America, research was limited to a single *comune*; a *comune* being an administrative unit (or municipality) incorporating both the village(s) and the adjacent countryside. The commune was located in the region of Calabria, a major source of immigrants to North America in the period of study, 1880 to 1930. As well as consulting standard written sources, it was planned that field work would be undertaken and oral testimony collected.[10]

The commune of Rende in southwestern Cosenza province was selected for the study and research was conducted there in addition to Toronto and Chicago, the main destinations of its emigrants to North America. However, discussions with informants, augmented by Italian sources, soon revealed a field of daily contact considerably wider than the *comune*. It became evident that, through the period of mass migration, there existed beyond the commune a unit of socio-economic interaction, often face-to-face, that was roughly bounded by a ten kilometre radius from Rende.[11] Geographically, this unit incorporating Rende and its eight surrounding *comuni* was termed the ''Rende area'' and it was within this area that interaction between individuals comprised what the French historian, Alain Morel, has called the ''social space'' of the inhabitants.[12] Basically, the spatial parameters of the Rende area corresponded to the distance a person could walk in one day and still return home. Collectively the people from this local area often referred to themselves as *paesani*.

This notion of an empirically grounded ''local area'' and its concomitant social space is significant. Although with large-scale emigration, one can no longer speak of a coherent geographic entity defined by *paesani*, the social space that people occupied within this small-scale unit does not evaporate, but rather withstands the trans-oceanic voyage to determine the pattern of human relations in the New World. Moving outward from a territorially bound local space in the Old World, then, one concludes with a socially determined space in the New, defined by the villagers' collective *mentalità*. This relationship between the Old World and the New is mediated of course by the phenomenon of chain migration and it is to its starting point — the geographic local space and the interaction of its villagers — to which we now turn by documenting, in some detail, the case of Rende.

EMIGRATION FROM RENDE AREA, 1881-97

Commune	Population Present * 1881	Emigration 1884	1885	1886	1887	1889	1890	1891	1892	1894	1895	1896	1897	Total Emigration (excluding 1888 & '93)	Total Emigrants as % of 1881 Pop.
Castiglione Cosentino	1,447	37	5	58	—	52	38	51	69	29	51	33	—	423	29.2
Castrolibero **	1,462	11	—	—	—	—	—	12	—	—	—	—	—	23	1.6
Cerisano	2,285	14	40	46	41	41	34	25	70	63	12	33	41	460	20.1
Marano Marchesato	2,757	17	47	20	34	16	40	29	34	21	16	67	16	357	13.0
Marano Principato **	1,365	—	—	—	—	17	—	—	—	—	—	21	—	38	2.8
Montalto Uffugo	6,013	152	183	95	—	220	49	43	67	57	123	26	—	1015	16.9
Rende	5,250	83	102	86	51	77	42	35	92	70	70	120	94	922	17.6
San Fili	3,760	83	175	110	144	105	118	102	143	55	68	68	44	1215	32.3
San Vincenzo la Costa	2,125	32	82	72	109	36	48	46	37	93	88	59	—	702	33.0
Total for Rende Area	26,464	429	634	487	378	564	369	343	512	388	428	427	195	5145	19.4
Total for District of Cosenza	174,591	1433	3386	2712	2607	2178	2919	2199	1707	1592	2682	1930	1576	21763	12.5

SOURCES: Ministero di Agricoltura, Industria e Commercio, Direzione Generale della Statistica, *Statistica della emigrazione italiana* for the years 1886 (p. 54), 1887 (p. 48), 1888 (p. 142), 1890 (p. 52), 1892 (p. 56), 1894-95 (p. 55), 1897 (p. 56).

* The "legally resident" population of the Rende area in 1881 was 27,890 (and 187,319 for Conseza district).

** Emigration figures incomplete.

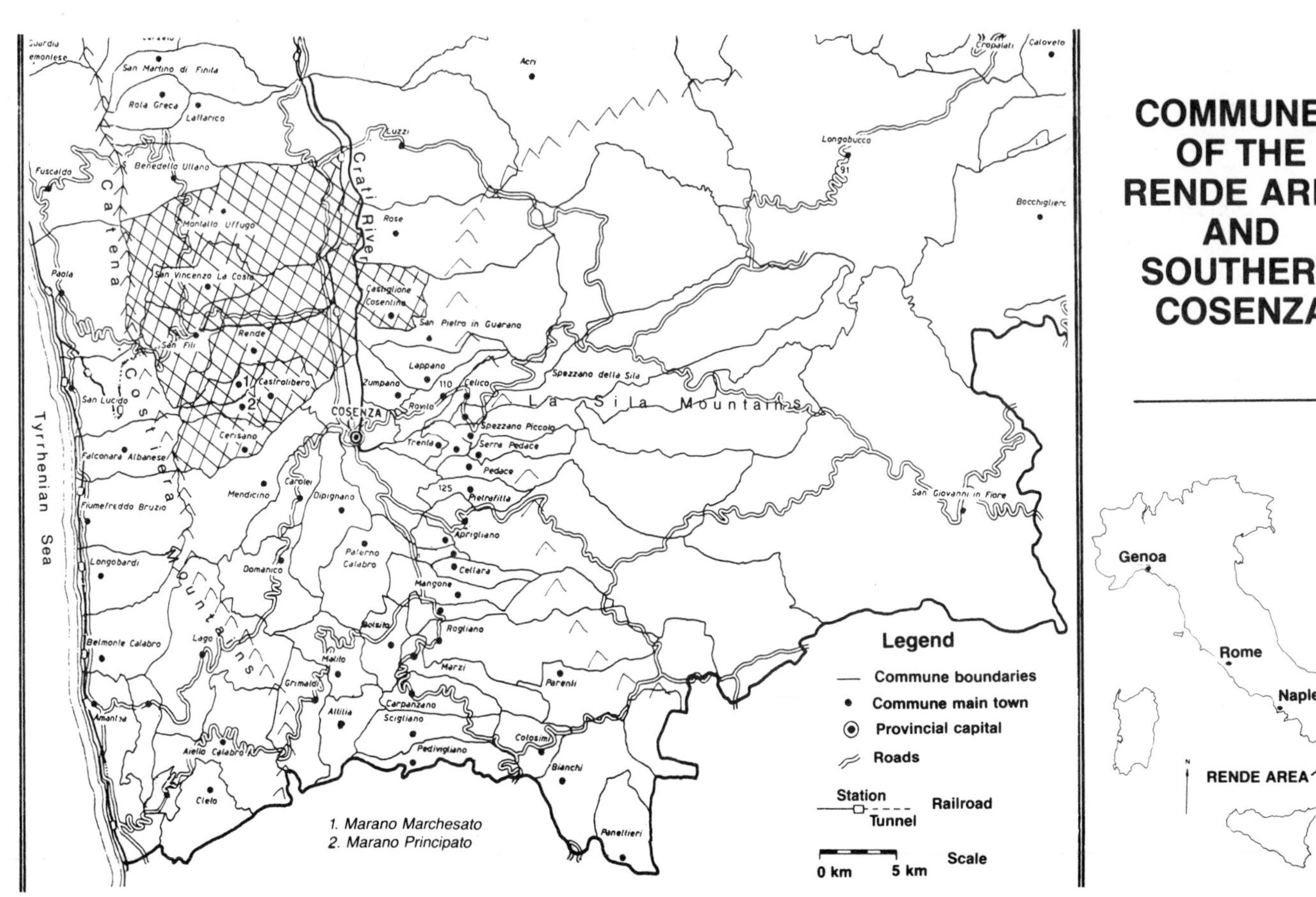
COMMUNES OF THE RENDE AREA AND SOUTHERN COSENZA
Legend
Commune boundaries
Commune main town
Provincial capital
Roads
Station
Tunnel
Railroad
0 km
5 km
Scale
1. Marano Marchesato
2. Marano Principato
Genoa
Rome
Naples
RENDE AREA
Cosenza
N
Tyrrhenian Sea
Catena Costiera Mountains
La Sila Mountains
Crati River
COSENZA
San Martino di Finita
Rota Greca
Lattarico
Fuscaldo
Benedetto Ullano
Montalto Uffugo
Paola
San Vincenzo La Costa
San Fili
Rende
Castrolibero
San Lucido
Cerisano
Falconara Albanese
Mendicino
Carolei
Dipignano
Fiumefreddo Bruzio
Longobardi
Domanico
Paterno Calabro
Belmonte Calabro
Lago
Malito
Grimaldi
Altilia
Amantea
Aiello Calabro
Cleto
Luzzi
Rose
Castiglione Cosentino
San Pietro in Guarano
Lappano
Zumpano
Rovito
Celico
110
Spezzano della Sila
Spezzano Piccolo
Trenta
Serra Pedace
Pedace
125
Pietrafitta
Aprigliano
Cellara
Mangone
Figline
Rogliano
Marzi
Parenti
Carpanzano
Scigliano
Pedivigliano
Colosimi
Bianchi
Panettieri
Acri
Longobucco
91
Cropalati
Caloveto
Bocchigliero
San Giovanni in Fiore

The Rende Area as an Illustrative Case

In 1881, the commune of Rende consisted of four villages and the town of Rende itself. It encompassed an area of 4,806 hectares and had a population, covering both nucleated settlements and countryside, of 5,250. As the seat of municipal government and as a religious and judicial centre the walled town of Rende played an important role in the lives of the local populace. In terms of the Rende area as a whole there existed considerable variation in the size of the nine *comuni* comprising the territory, though on the eve of mass emigration its population totalled 26,464.[13]

Social and economic links tied the commune of Rende to surrounding municipalities within a longitudinally oval-shaped area bounded on the east by the watershed of the Catena Costiera Mountains and on the west by the Crati River, the most important waterway in Calabria. Although the communes of the Rende area encompassed over two dozen towns, villages and hamlets, geographically the area was quite small, and hence interaction was relatively easy. It was only six kilometers from the town of Rende eastward to San Fili and about twelve kilometers northward to the furthest town, Montalto. A short distance of eleven kilometers separated Rende from the provincial capital of Cosenza to the southeast. And from the centre of the commune to the more distant of the neighbouring *comuni*, it was only a few hours' walk.

Within the Rende area there existed considerable economic interaction which made it an entity. Peasants in the fertile low-lying areas of Rende who specialized in intensive vegetable cultivation sold their produce in the town markets of the higher placed communes to the east

(San Fili and San Vincenzo la Costa), where local production could not meet the demand. In turn, the peasants of these communes exploited the abundant forests within their realms and sold chestnuts — used for both animal and human consumption — and charcoal to the inhabitants of Rende. Especially after the elimination of municipal levies on local area goods and produce in the 1880s, trade between the *comuni* of the Rende area improved.[14]

The important agricultural fair of Arcavacata, held annually at the end of August just north of the town of Rende, also acted to bring together the population of the Crati Valley in a hectic week of buying and selling. The fair dealt heavily with livestock, particularly cattle, and though much of this originated in the mountain pastures of the La Sila Mountains just east of the Rende area, agriculturalists from the higher placed communes of San Fili, San Vincenzo and western Montalto also participated as sellers. Most of the peasants of the Rende area however attended the fair as buyers. Purchases were usually made of young animals to be fattened over the winter months and later used either for the peasant's own consumption or to be sold on the urban market, Cosenza taking a large share of the supply. While the Arcavacata fair was of particular importance to the Rende area, it also attracted participants and buyers from all over the province and as far away as Crotone, Reggio Calabria and even Naples.

Very much connected with the economic linkage that occurred among *comuni* was the fact that the more powerful landlords often owned estates that straddled two, three, or more communes. In the late nineteenth century, for example, the Magdalone family, which had extensive holdings in Rende and dominated its economic life, also held land in neighbouring Marano Marchesato.[15] In such cases where *comuni* were brought under the common economic dealings of large landlords, their inhabitants often came into contact with each other both socially and economically in various ways. For instance, labourers could be allocated from one commune to another by the landlord, depending on labour needs at the time, thus intermingling the municipal populations. And the landlord's teamsters, while transporting the produce of the various enterprises of the landlord, criss-crossed municipalities and played the important role of carriers of information from peasants in one commune to those in another.

Ties of a primarily social nature paralleled economic links in binding peasants together. Some of these social contacts revolved around the peasants' religion, which on an intra-communal level, provided opportunities for close interaction among the various sections or neighbourhoods of the individual communes. Throughout Rende, the second largest municipality after Montalto, there were about a dozen churches. The major churches were located within the town itself while about half were spread throughout the countryside. Rather than adhering to a single neighbourhood church as was common in North America, people frequented the various churches according to their preferred hour or day of service since different ones held mass at different times. Worshippers would also go beyond their neighbourhood in order to participate in the various religious *feste* for which particular churches were responsible. Hence, for example, families who regarded San Michele as a patron saint (and after whom the families' patriarch and other males would often be named) would converge every eighth of May at the Chiesa del Ritiro, responsible for the celebration of the saint's day and procession.[16]

Though such mixing served to integrate the inhabitants of the various sections of Rende, on the intercommunal level, travel between communes in order to partake in neighbouring *feste* was common and facilitated social contacts among the peasantry of the Rende area as a whole. It frequently happened, for example, that the people of Rende would travel to the neighbouring *comune* of Marano Principato in order to celebrate the important feast of the Madonna del Carmine (Our Lady of Mount Carmel) in July. Travelling outside the Rende area, it was usual for the peasants of the area to make an annual pilgrimage across the eastern mountains to the renowned monastery of San Francesco da Paola. On week-ends and holidays young single men in couples or in small groups would walk to Castiglione, San Fili, Montalto, Cosenza, or even Paola, to pass away idle hours in the town square, perhaps buy an ice or lemon drink, or sometimes visit relatives or friends.

While such excursions could occasionally lead to the chance meeting of young women and intermarriage between communes, marrying outside one's municipality was more usually linked with internal migration within the Rende area. This migration was agriculturally based and took two forms. First, men, as well as women and children, would seek out seasonal work harvesting in the summer or sowing in the autumn in the large wheat-growing estates of the lower-lying half of the Rende area. Often such agricultural workers would migrate eastward beyond the Rende area to the extensive wheat estates of the Crotone plain, the vineyards of Rossano, or the mountain valleys of La Sila for the sowing or harvesting of rye, potatoes, or corn.[17]

Second, and more likely to lead to intermarriage, was

the movement of young single men from the more mountainous and rugged parts of the area where land holdings were small and often fragmented to the less congested plains where an attempt was made to rent land on a long-term stable basis. One peasant *fattore* (factor), who worked for a medium-scale landlord married off three of his four daughters to such young men from outside Rende. One of these young men was from Marano Principato and had settled on the estate as a tenant. The second, as a boy, had followed his family, which migrated from the north and settled near the estate on the land of another landowner. The third spouse was the nephew of the Marano settler who met his wife on one of his regular visits to his uncle.

Though intermarriage occurred mainly through the in-migration of men, instances where Rende males married outside women who then joined their husbands in the commune were not infrequent. And, of course, out-migration from Rende also occurred. For example, one young man found prosperity by leaving the *comune* to marry and take land as a dowry in the village of San Sisto (within the neighbouring municipality of San Vincenzo). Migration and intermarriage were also facilitated by major public works as in the case of the spur railroad line built around World War I through Rende and San Fili in order to connect the city of Cosenza with the main line along the coast at Paola.[18] The work attracted to the two communes construction workers not only from the Rende area but also from neighbouring regions.

While migration and intermarriage bound families throughout the Rende area together, these factors influenced the various communes through the "fellow-villager" relationship. Migrants who entered a commune from the neighbouring municipalities and who intermarried and settled there were eventually regarded as fellow-villagers, or *paesani* in its narrow municipal sense. But since these people were simultaneously still regarded as fellow-villagers in their communes of origin, they often acted to bind socially the populations of their original and adopted *comuni* through various social contacts: visiting, attending weddings or baptisms, and the like.

Through these various connections between *comuni*, families were known throughout the Rende area. Though obviously not all individuals within the area had personal contact with each other, people's reputations as reflected by their family membership and as transmitted through key intermediaries such as migrants or local merchants were widely known. Sometimes a family's reputation was reflected in the very nickname by which it was known and commonly the *soprannome* took the place of surnames among the peasantry. As an area of common reputation, as a "moral community," an additional criterion of unity was given to the Rende area.[19]

While it has been argued that the Rende area formed one cohesive socio-economic unit, this should not be misconstrued to mean that differences and competition between *comuni* did not exist. Each had its own municipal pride, its own patron saint, and even dress.[20] And though each tried to assert its identity in a positive way, the reputation by which any individual commune was known often took on a humorously derogatory flavour (as was sometimes the case with family nicknames) which reflected the rivalry among them for social standing. Hence while both Rende and San Fili had reputations for being sly, another *comune* was said to be composed of "country bumpkins" whose inhabitants walked about dumbly with open mouths (''*bocche-aperte*''). Yet another commune was known by the name of the wide skirts its women wore, while Cosenza was thought to be a city of loose women. Nevertheless, though conflict existed, the socio-economic links between municipalities successfully countervailed the rivalry among them. Especially in the case of internal migration and intermarriage the ties that were forged between people were both immediate and durable. With emigration to the New World ties among people from the Rende area became more extensive and more manifest, and were utilized to facilitate both the processes of emigration and settlement.

The influence of kinship as a major operational component — alongside social space — giving shape and drive to migration chains has been dealt with elsewhere and need not be detailed here.[21] It will suffice to point out that within the Rende area the nature of kinship was considerably different from the familism, that is the narrow self-interest of the nuclear family, that forms part and parcel of a number of academic characterizations of the Italian South. Rather, the reality within the Rende area was consonant with an alternative view that stresses the cohesion of the wider kindred, the importance of friends and neighbours, and the intricate system of rights and obligations binding individuals to one another.[22] At the associational level this bonding was most clearly witnessed in the formation of agricultural work parties and the celebration of rites of passage ranging from baptisms to funerals. There can be little doubt that the cohesion of the wider kindred facilitated migration through the dissemination of information and mutual aid — such as the forwarding of steamship tickets, extending of accommodation, or caring of families left behind.

Implications

Having presented a view of local area and social space as fundamental in determining the scale of migration chains, it is fitting that some discussion be offered as to how this impinges on the migration process. Three aspects of migration will be addressed: padronism, immigrant settlement, and chain diversion. The evidence here is by no means final and the following is presented as suggestive of further research rather than as conclusive.

As in the literature dealing with chain migration, the question of scale is often implicitly, if not explicitly, found in the rather substantial, and growing, body of work on padronism.[23] While it is true that the recruitment of adult labourers could range from the local greengrocer who sponsored a few relatives and *compari* to agents like Montreal's Antonio Cordasco who imported men in the thousands from throughout the peninsula, nonetheless the question of representativeness remains. In the case of Rende area emigrants, at least, a pattern quite consonant with the parameters of scale discussed above emerges.[24]

At the turn of the century, there were at least three *padroni* from the Rende area in Chicago, the major magnet of *paesani*, who were sponsoring the immigration of labourers. Luigi Spizzirri, Francesco Principe and Giuliano Sicilia were well known men of considerable power who could supply *paesani* with loans and work, as well as mediate between them and North American society. In the much smaller colony of Toronto, Salvatore Turano from San Sisto, who owned a grocery cum boarding-house on Mansfield Avenue, played a similar role as labour agent.[25]

It is interesting to note that three of these *padroni*

came from the most mountainous, hardest pressed communes, that is to say, those which had the earliest outmigration. Yet it is significant that they acted not only as intermediaries for men from their own *comuni*, but for the Rende area as a whole. The socio-economic linkages that bound the Rende area into a cohesive unit — intermarriage and kinship, common *feste*, and markets — were utilized by villagers to gain information regarding the *padroni* and make contact with them. The individual peasant-emigrant learned whom to see in the New World through the informal personal networks that linked kinsmen and friends throughout the Rende area. Just as the reputations of peasants and local intermediaries were widely known and were part of the day-to-day interaction between villagers, so too were the names and deeds of the New World *padroni*.

Of the Rende area *padroni*, Luigi Spizzirri from San Vincenzo emerged as the most influential. Arriving in Chicago as a young man in the early 1870s he was instrumental in stimulating the heavy emigration that materialized in the 1880s from the Rende area, as well as Cosenza more generally. In addition to running an employment agency, Spizzirri owned related immigrant businesses — boarding-house, grocery, saloon, bank, and steamship agency — located on South Clark Street in Chicago's early Little Italy. Further, he was an officer of two mutual benefit societies, the Bersaglieri di Savoia and the Società Cristoforo Colombo. There is little doubt that Spizzirri, as labour agent and otherwise, rose beyond his own circle of *paesani* to prominence within the more general Calabrian immigrant community.[26] To a lesser extent, a similar branching out could be detected in the careers of the other *padroni*. But none became a Cordasco.

The basis of their enterprise remained the Rende area *paesani* and it was upon this that their success, whether modest or substantial, was built. Moreover, even in the case of Luigi Spizzirri, for the peasant-emigrant anxious to seek his fortune in America, his New World contact was not Spizzirri, the big-time *padrone*, but Spizzirri the *paesano*, whose reputation was known.

In dealing with immigrant settlement patterns recent microstudies by Vecoli for Chicago, Zucchi for Toronto and Baily for Buenos Aires, among others, have done much to dispell the image of a homogeneous "Little Italy" inserted within the urban landscape.[27] It is now clear that chain migration was translated into chain residence patterns. The clustering of immigrants from particular locales around pioneers or earlier settled kin and *paesani* was evidently more decisive as a factor of settlement than proximity to work, access to services, or even the market value of accommodation (though, obviously, all were interwoven).

Here again the Rende area experience suggests that in determining the shape of specific immigrant clusters, in determining the extent of operational linkage and interpersonal interaction; or to state it otherwise, in defining the extent of community in its *gemeinschaft* sense, it may be more useful to think in terms of local area connections than of *campanilismo* or *regionalismo*.[28]

Although after World War I, Rende area immigrants formed part of the major Little Italy that emerged in Chicago's Near West Side, within this, the *paesani* occupied a well defined neighbourhood centred on Miller Street, and regarded themselves as distinct. Within the Rende area concentration, there was a constant to and fro of visiting, male *paesani* played *bocce* or *scoppa* and women participated in sewing and baking circles. Work parties were formed for the renovation of homes and around the making of wine and *salsiccia* and *soppressata* in the autumn. Where there was to be a money transaction, it was preferable to frequent the groceries, shoe repairs or tailor shops of *paesani* rather than those of others. Where possible, people went to work in factories, warehouses, railroad yards and on construction sites in known groups. And while they attended the Church of Our Lady of Pompei, it was the feast day of San Francesco da Paola that was most enthusiastically celebrated by *paesani*.

This camaraderie and identification with local area was repeated in the smaller College Street Little Italy of Toronto. Here, near the main intersection at Grace Street, Salvatore Turano's grocery/boarding-house and agency on Mansfield Avenue attracted a growing number of *paesani*, especially with redevelopment in the original receiving area of St. John's Ward after 1911. Moreover, as recognized by Zucchi, who makes the perceptive distinction between marriage within "hometown" groups — at which level endogamy may not seem particularly significant — and marriage within the local area cluster, in the latter case, the rate of endogamy can be impressive indeed. Hence, in his examination of 43 immigrants from *comuni* in the Rende area, whereas about 35 % of his sample married immigrants from their respective hometowns, around 61 % married within the Rende area group.[29] In the New World, as was true in the Old, Rende area endogamy among *paesani* was an enduring index of the reality of a local social space. Such endogamy tended to extend — along with rites of passage celebrations and numerous other interactions — the *paesani*'s sense of social space beyond the immigrant generation and neighbourhood base.

Of all the themes subsumed by the study of migration, perhaps the least attention has been given to the question of chain diversion. While chains had specific key destinations, the strength of a target's pull could ebb, causing the movement to change course. Moreover, simultaneous to the major flow from a particular locale, there was always a general fall-out for sundry reasons to various minor destinations, towards which rivulets might be directed by specific links of kinship, occupation, communal fellowship, or combinations of these. Within a particular migratory field, it could happen that if a major target was for some reason blocked, because of political or economic constraints, for instance, then one of the minor concentrations could be called upon by potential emigrants and itself emerge as a prime destination. Such a dynamic arose as part of the Rende area story.[30]

In the late nineteenth century, emigration from southwestern Cosenza averaged close to 2,000 per annum, almost a quarter of which was from the Rende area. Though North America, especially Chicago, received a considerable part of this outflow, in fact, it was the Southern Hemisphere, and in particular Buenos Aires, that attracted the majority of emigrants. Drawn by Argentina's "Golden Age," these emigrants, about 80 % of whom were male sojourners, went to work as agricultural labourers in the wheat fields, as peddlers and artisans, or more commonly, as railroad navvies.

At the turn of the century, economic recession in Argentina juxtaposed with unprecedented industrial growth and high wages in the United States, resulted in the diversion of a majority of the growing exodus from southwestern Cosenza — which averaged over 7,500 emigrants per year after 1904 — towards the northern Republic. The fact that Chicago was the transportation hub of the continent and contained known Rende area *padroni* attracted *paesani* and especially the many sojourners who sought seasonal, readily available work on the numerous railroad lines that fanned out from the Windy City. The fact that the city offered a variety of jobs in the construction of its urban transportation infrastructure, or in factories and mills, or in small retail stores of its Little Italies, appealed to the increasing minority that was deciding to settle permanently in the New Land.

Emigration was, of course, interrupted by World War I, and while the earlier mass volume was again reached by 1920, the revival was short-lived. American restrictionist legislation aimed at curtailing southeastern European immigration was introduced in 1921 and made even more severe in 1924. Through a system of quotas, Italian immigration was reduced to a mere few thousand per annum. For the second time in less than two generations *paesani* were forced to consider an alternative to their established trajectory. This alternative involved the use of the small Toronto colony as a bridgehead for a diversion northward into Canada, though the resultant deflection was itself soon cut short by the Great Depression and restrictionism on the part of both the Canadian and Italian governments. Numerically, this movement, as worked out in the 1920s, was but a fraction of the Chicago stream. Nonetheless, it was of great significance since it established the ground for the mass immigration of *paesani* to Toronto in the post-World War II era.

The earliest Rende area settlers in Toronto were most likely fruit traders, especially from San Vincenzo la Costa and Montalto Uffugo, who had established themselves in the southern part of "the Ward" by the 1880s.[31] The fledgling colony was steadily augmented by newcomers; particularly labourers who followed work from the United States into Ontario. There they were employed by firms like the Canadian Pacific and Grand Trunk railroads in the bush, after which they made their way to their Toronto *paesani*. Throughout the 1920s the earlier established settlers from the communes of San Vincenzo la Costa (especially the village of San Sisto) and Montalto Uffugo, were utilized by people from the entire Rende area to gain access into the Dominion. Since Italian immigration to Canada during the decade was basically limited to those considered "agriculturalists," it was necessary for potential immigrants to seek out kinsmen and friends who could see to the processing of official documents and other matters necessary to have them enter as farm labourers.[32]

This dynamic of diversion and its relation to social space can best be understood by tracing individuals belonging to a specific chain segment. Consider two of the Chiappetta brothers from San Vincenzo. After working as railroad labourers in the eastern and mid-western states at the turn of the century, the two men made their way through Buffalo to Toronto, where they were joined by a third brother. From their commune of origin, the kinship ties of the Chiappettas stretched southward to Marano Marchesato, where they had a sister who married into the Ruffalo family. In the early part of the century, the brothers sponsored one of their Marano nephews, thus placing in Toronto a contact whom other potential emigrants from the *comune* could utilize when needed. Further, the Marano immigrant was related through his sister's marriage to the Cosentino family of Rende. When the Rende couple decided to emigrate, the role of sponsor fell, in turn, on Ruffalo; that is, the nearest kin able to provide aid. In any case, it can be seen that the settlement in Toronto of a single family from San Vincenzo carried with it kinship ties extending to at least two other Rende area communes.

This pattern of intervillage and kinship linkages was repeated in several other chain segments. Similar interpersonal linkages, for example, connected Rende immigrants to Castiglione and San Fili. The phenomenon was a common occurrence, not an exception. Concretely, with the coming of restrictionism such networks meant that, once the potential emigrant had shifted his gaze from the Republic to the Dominion, even if he did not personally know a Toronto sponsor, he had access to a circle of Rende area contacts from which he could draw to expedite his immigration. Moreover, the twenties movement was illustrative of the resilience of peasant-emigrants in effecting a major change in the direction and organization of their chain migration in response to modern, bureaucratic controls on their movement and purpose.

It can be stated that in the case of the Rende area *paesani*, what could appear on the surface as separate village chains were often interlocking movements defined by the parameters of a Rende area social space. With the advent of restrictionism, the diversion of chain migration was made possible by the reality of this social space and the interconnecting network of *comuni* and kindred it encompassed.

Conclusion

Having raised the question of scale in the study of Italian chain migration, it has been this paper's purpose to place some parameters on the extent of the interconnections comprising such movement. The concept of a local area social space was discussed as giving shape to chain migration and providing the dynamic driving its movement.

Addressing the question of scale can act as an important point of entry in understanding the physical, social and psychological world of Italian emigrants and can provide new insight into the New World experience. The paper dealt schematically with the implications of scale for padronism, settlement and chain diversion, although much more could have been written along the same lines about associational life, occupational chains and other major topics of immigrant settlement. Indeed, it can be said that the question of scale has implications for the very definition of "ethnicity;" the term being defined from the perspective of the participants vis-à-vis the observers, rather than the reverse: defined as a matter of group self-identification rather than elite perception.

To the extent that this discussion has sparked some interest as to what precisely we mean when speaking of Italian "chain migration," to the extent that it prompts us to look beyond the chain image to its substance and significant implications, it has fulfilled its purpose.

NOTES

1. Adolfo Rossi, "Vantaggi e danni dell'emigrazione nel mezzogiorno d'Italia (Note di un viaggio fatto in Basilicata e in Calabria)," *Bolletino dell'Emigrazione*, no. 13 (Rome, 1908), 1549-1645; Benedetto Croce, *Storia del regno di Napoli* (Bari, 1925, reprint ed., 1966), 341 ff.; Broughton Brandenburg, *Imported Americans: The Story of A Disguised American and his wife studying the Emigration Question* (New York, 1904), 101, 238; Robert T. Park and Herbert A. Miller, *Old World Traits Transplated* (New York, 1921), 146-59. For early Northern Italian immigration chains based on specific trades in the mid-nineteenth century, see Charles MacFarlane, *Popular Customs, Sports, and Recollections of the South of Italy*, chapter entitled "Wandering Italians" (London, 1846), 135-51.

2. John S. MacDonald and Leatrice D. MacDonald, "Chain Migration, Ethnic Neighbourhood Formation, and Social Networks," *Milbank Memorial Fund Quarterly* 42 (1964), 82-97; John S. MacDonald and Leatrice D. MacDonald, "Italian Migration to Australia: Manifest Functions of Bureaucracy Versus Latent Functions of Informal Networks," *Journal of Social History* 3, 3 (Spring 1970), 249-75; Charles A. Price, "Southern Europeans in Australia: Problems of Assimilation," *International Migration Review* 2, 3 (Summer 1968), 3-24; Trevor R. Lee, "The Role of the Ethnic Community as a Reception Area for Italian Immigrants in Melbourne, Australia," *International Migration* 8, 1-2 (1970), 50-63.

3. John S. MacDonald, "Italy's Rural Social Structure and Migration," *Occidente* 12, 5 (September 1956), 437-56; John S. MacDonald, "Some Socio-economic Emigration Differentials in Rural Italy, 1902-1913," *Economic Change and Cultural Change* 7, 1 (October 1958), 55-72; John S. MacDonald, "Agricultural Organization, Migration and Labour Militancy in Rural Italy," *Economic History Review* 16, 1-3 (1963-64), 61-75; John S. MacDonald and Leatrice D. MacDonald, "Urbanization, Ethnic Groups, and Social Segmentation," *Social Research* 29, 4 (Winter 1962), 433-48.

4. MacDonald, "Chain Migration," 82.

5. An exception is provided by Samuel L. Baily, "Chain migration of Italians to Argentina: case studies of the Agnonesi and the Sirolesi," *Studi Emigrazione* XIX, 65 (March 1982), 73-91. A recent analysis which extends the chain migration model by examining how early itinerant tradesmen influenced the choice of destination was recently presented by John E. Zucchi, "Precursors of the 'New Immigration'; Italian Street Musicians 1815-1885," paper presented for the Elia Chair in Italian-Canadian Studies, York University, North York, Ontario, February, 1986. Also see William A. Douglass, *Emigration in a South Italian Town: An Anthropological History* (New Brunswick, N.J., 1984).

6. See Josef F. Barton, *Peasants and Strangers: Italians, Rumanians, and Slovaks in an American City, 1890-1950* (Cambridge, Mass., 1975), chap. 3; John W. Briggs, *An Italian Passage: Immigrants to Three American Cities, 1890-1930* (New Haven, 1978), chap. 5.

7. Leonard W. Moss and Stephen C. Cappannari, "Patterns of Kinship, Comparaggio and Community in a South Italian Village," *Anthropological Quarterly* 33 (1960), 24-32; Leonard W. Moss and Stephen C. Cappannari, "Estate and Class in a Southern Italian Hill Village," *American Anthropologist* 64, 2 (1962), 287-300.

8. Rudolph J. Vecoli, "Contadini in Chicago: A Critique of *The Uprooted*," *Journal of American History* LI (December 1964), 406.

9. Baily, "Chain Migration of Italians;" Rudolph M. Bell, *Fate and Honor, Family and Village: Demographic and Cultural Change in Rural Italy since 1800* (Chicago, 1979), chap. 7.

10. For a detailed account of the following analysis see Franc Sturino, "Inside the Chain: A Case Study in Southern Italian Migration to North America, 1880-1930" (Ph.D. Diss., University of Toronto, 1981), introduction and chap. 1, sec. 1. An excellent collection of essays on emigration from Calabria is provided by Pietro Borzomati, ed., *L'emigrazione calabrese dall'unità ad oggi* (Rome, 1982).

11. It should be noted that the range of a local area can vary depending on geography, the pull of a major centre, ease of communication and other factors. To cite but one example, in two instances where the origin of an immigrant grouping was described in terms of a cluster of villages, the range of contact was about twice the size of the Rende area *paesani*. Levitt, in describing Chicago's Sicilian "colony" in the early part of the century recognized that it did not originate from a single source, but rather from a cluster of villages in northern Palermo province. This cluster was roughly pivoted around Bagheria and about twice the size of the Rende area. Baily in his recent study of Sirolesi from the Marches in Buenos Aires suggests that the social space of the emigrants had extended as far as 18 kilometres.

In these two instances there exists a plausible explanation for the discrepancy in size vis-à-vis the Rende area. It is not unlikely that the difference resulted from the fact that the Sicilian and Marchiggiani clusters bordered the sea. This probably made communications among the coastal communes easier than had been true in the land-locked Rende area. Along the coast it was possible for communes lying within a more extensive territory to be brought into contact with each other forming the kind of interpersonal social space illustrated below for the Rende area, albeit on a wider scale. Marie Levitt, "Report on the Sicilian Colony in Chicago" (manuscript), cited in Park and Miller, *Old World Traits*, 151; Baily, "Chain Migration of Italians," 83-9.

12. Alain Morel, "L'espace social d'un village picard," *Études rurales* 45, 73 (1972), 62-80.

13. Italy, Ministero di Agricoltura, Industria e Commercio, Direzione Generale della Statistica, *Censimento della popolazione del regno d'Italia al 31 dicembre 1881*, 1, pt. 1: *Popolazione dei comuni e dei mandamenti* (Rome, 1883), 120-23.

14. Luigi Conforti, *Risposta all'opuscolo "Una provincia Fuori legge"* (Cosenza, 1881), 19-23.

15. *Ibid.*, 63-65.

16. Gerardo Giraldi, *Le chiese di Rende: itinerario storico-artistico* (Cosenza, 1985); Touring Club Italiano, *Basilicata e Calabria*, 3rd ed. (Milano, 1965), 407-08. Note that while Michaelmas falls on September 29th, May 8th is the date of the appari-

tion of St. Michael the Archangel to San Francesco da Paola, the chief saint of Cosenza, and San Gennaro.

17. D. Taruffi, L. De Nobili, C. Lori, *La Questione agraria e l'emigrazione in Calabria* (Firenze, 1908), 137-38.

18. Ilario Principe, *La Calabria* (Firenze, 1968), 144-45.

19. F.G. Bailey, "The Peasant View of the Bad Life," in *Peasant and Peasant Society*, ed. Teodor Shanin (Harmondsworth, Eng., 1971), 302-03. Cf. J.A. Pitt-Rivers, *The People of the Sierra* (Chicago, 1961), 160 ff.

20. The English writer and painter, Arthur John Strutt, for example, travelling through Calabria in the late nineteenth century, documented the distinctive dress and flavour of various villages. Luigi Parpagliolo, "La Calabria negli scrittori straniere," *Almanacco Calabrese* 1, 1 (1950), 94, 101-2.

21. Franc Sturino, "Family and Kin Cohesion among South Italian Immigrants in Toronto," in *The Italian Immigrant Woman in North America*, eds. Betty B. Caroli, Robert F. Harney and Lydio F. Tomasi (Toronto, 1978), 288-311.

22. Edward C. Banfield, *The Moral Basis of a Backward Society* (New York, 1958) presents the standard view of "amoral familism." An alternative perspective is offered by Jan Brögger, *Montevarese: A Study of Peasant Society and Culture in Southern Italy* (Oslo, 1971) and John Davis, *Land and Family in Pisticci* (London, 1973).

23. Robert F. Harney, "The Padrone and the Immigrant," *Canadian Review of American Studies* 5, 2 (Fall 1974), 101-18; Robert F. Harney, "The Commerce of Migration," *Canadian Ethnic Studies* 9, 1 (1977), 42-53; Robert F. Harney, "Montreal's King of Italian Labour: A Case Study of Padronism," *Labour/Le Travail* 4 (1979), 57-84; Bruno Ramirez and Michael Del Balso, *The Italians of Montreal: From Sojourning to Settlement 1900-1921* (Montreal, 1980); Bruno Ramirez, *Les premiers Italiens de Montréal: L'origine de la Petite Italie du Québec* (Montréal, 1984), chap. 2. Among the many American studies on padronism, see Humbert S. Nelli, *The Italians in Chicago 1880-1930* (New York, 1970), chap. 3; Luciano J. Iorizzo, "The Padrone and Immigrant Distribution," in *The Italian Experience in the United States*, eds. Silvano M. Tomasi and Madelaine H. Engel (New York, 1970), 43-75.

To give but one example of the confusion in the minds of contemporaneous observers regarding the padrone's level of activity, the American Immigration Commission in the space of a few paragraphs saw the scale of padronism as being defined by "race," fellow "countrymen," "sectional prejudices," and "provincial boundary lines." *Reports of the United States Immigration Commission*, 37 (Washington, 1911), 216-18.

24. Sturino, "Inside the Chain," 313-39.

25. See John E. Zucchi, "Italian Hometown Settlements and the Development of an Italian Community in Toronto, 1875-1935," in *Gathering Place: Peoples and Neighbourhoods of Toronto*, ed. Robert F. Harney (Toronto, 1985), 123, 126.

26. Rudoph J. Vecoli, "Chicago's Italians Prior to World War I: A Study of their Social and Economic Adjustment" (Ph.D. Diss., University of Wisconsin, 1963), 105, 253-60; Giovanni E. Schiavo, *The Italians in Chicago: A Study in Americanization* (Chicago, 1928), 55-56.

27. Rudolph J. Vecoli, "The Formation of Chicago's Little Italies," *Journal of American Ethnic History* 2, 2 (Spring 1983), 5-20; Zucchi, "Italian Hometown Settlements"; Baily, "Chain Migration of Italians." Among other relevant studies are Lee, "The Role of the Ethnic Community" and J.H. Burnley, "Italian Migration and Settlement in New Zealand, 1874-1968," *International Migration* 9, 3-4 (1971), 139-55.

28. Sturino, "Inside the Chain," 438-56, 565-82.

29. Zucchi, "Italian Hometown Settlements," 139.

30. Sturino, "Inside the Chain," chap. 6, sec. 1. See also chap. 2, sec. 2.

31. Zucchi, "Italian Hometown Settlements," 131.

32. Details on this phase of emigration can be found in Franc Sturino, "Italian immigration to Canada and the farm labour system through the 1920's," *Studi Emigrazione* XXII, 77 (March 1985), 81-97.

Canada as a Target of Trade and Emigration in Post-Unification Italian Writing

Nicoletta Serio *

The Italian press after Unification in 1870 played an increasingly important role in the spread of news from foreign countries, especially that which concerned travel, exploration, technological advances, emigration, and achievements in social welfare and education. This accumulation of information could have formed an intellectual foundation for solving the social and economic problems of a country that achieved unification before its industrial revolution. But the Italian ruling class was generally unresponsive to this stimulus. Yet the dissemination of this information did help Italians to create an imaginary map of the possible targets of emigration and make known to them the life and institutions of the countries of the New World.

* Translated by Gabriella Colussi.

The interest in North America shown by post-Unification Italians had a very different focus from the writings of the seventeenth and eighteenth centuries. Previously, voyages of exploration and the creation of English, French and Spanish colonies had captured the imagination of the Italian general public, especially through the anthropological and naturalistic descriptions which were provided. On the other hand, the colonial conflicts occurring on the North American continent aroused interest because of their implications for European stability.[1]

In the latter part of the nineteenth century, even the British North American colonies did not escape the attention of Italian writers who were particularly interested in the economic relationship between the colonies and the mother country in light of the United States' policy censuring the use of force to maintain colonial ties. Although an isolated proposal in its time, Cristoforo Negri suggested in 1863 the possibility of direct trade relations between New Brunswick and Italy, since Great Britain was no longer able to maintain her privileges in the trade between Europe and Canada. Negri regretted the fact that no Italian ship had reached the ports of New Brunswick,

> ... in spite of the fact that Cabot introduced those seas and regions to the world and that from official [English] charts it appears that various imported goods originating from Italy arrive on foreign ships and that export goods from Canada are sent to Italy on English and American ships. We, therefore, lose the advantages of direct trade, and yield profits to other nations.[2]

Negri then listed the Italian products that would be

well received in Canada and the Canadian natural resources that Italy would find advantageous to import. His underlying assumption throughout was that both countries would benefit from an improved knowledge of their respective industrial activities.

> Canadians have the largest deep sea fishing industries in the world: they are consumers of salt and oils; they use, but do not produce, silks and wines and they import quantities of dried fruit. There is wealth and luxury in that country. Our marbles, our works of Florentine, Genoese and Neapolitan art would surely not be neglected... Our know-how would in time help Canadian industry [in naval construction and other activities] and all this would become very profitable for us.[3]

Negri clearly understood that the Canadian colonies were undergoing a rapid and impressive development; this progressive and peaceful growth was very different from the United States', which went from a revolution to civil war. As a scholar of colonization and emigration he admired the,

> ... rapidity in growth of those Canadian colonies. Strengthened by the people of Europe that emigrate yearly, the colonies undergo an unfettered and active expansion on clear and free land, upon which the seeds of slavery had never taken root.[4]

Negri's studies and activities made him particularly sensitive to the problem of emigration and foreign trade. After 1848, he was director of the Department of Emigration of the Kingdom of Sardinia and, subsequently, director of the Kingdom's consulates for which he compiled a code. He was president of the Italian Geographical Society and established the *Bollettino Consolare* for the registration of Italians abroad.[5] According to Negri, "it was imperative to know, after the unification of so many regions of Italy, the interests of all the Italians abroad, not only those of the Sardinians"[6] in order to decide where new consulates should be opened and how the older inefficient ones could be reorganized. He pointed out that the majority of Italian consulates in 1863 were not administered by Italians: of 125 consulates and 268 delegations or vice-consulates, only 43 of the former and 7 of the latter were assigned to civil servants sent from the Italian peninsula. The others were left in the hands of local agents often of foreign nationality.[7]

In addition, these agents "either have positions with the local government, are professionals there, or are merchants who compete with our seafarers."[8] In all cases, these people had greater relations and common interests with the host country than with Italy. For this reason the protection of Italian emigrants was often subject to negotiations between the local notables of the community and the politicians of the host country. Italy would acquire greater prestige abroad if it regulated such matters through formal negotiations at the international level.

From his studies of British colonization, Negri concluded that the Italian state should follow the example of Britain by encouraging and funding the initiatives of societies for geographic exploration, of navigation companies and of commercial enterprises, in the search for new markets and territories to colonize peacefully. At the same time the State should make use of the information collected by consuls and private citizens in order to direct Italian emigrants to places more suitable to them politically, economically, and climatically.

His proposals, however, were not well received in Italy since reflection on the strategies of colonization and on the opportunities of emigration was only just beginning. Even if the conquest of the New World was followed with interest in the years prior to Unification, this process was essentially seen as one of the expansion of European powers in search of raw materials to bolster their respective economies. In other words, Italians did not perceive the first phase of European colonization as a solution to the problems of overpopulation, of poverty, of political and religious conflict, or of social instability.

From the 1870s on, Italians began to rethink the process of British colonization, paying particular attention to these factors with a view to formulating a policy on emigration. It was no coincidence that these thoughts found expression in Leone Carpi's first study of Italian emigration which appeared after the Ministry of Internal Affairs granted the author permission to gather an initial set of data.[9] Carpi, who had been a member of the government of the Roman Republic in 1849 and was subsequently exiled, was one of the most important Italian scholars of immigration. His text *Delle colonie e dell'emigrazione d'Italiani all'estero sotto l'aspetto dell'industria commercio e agricoltura*, published in 1878, constitutes the first collection of documents and statistics concerning Italian emigration and remains to this day an essential source for the study of this phenomenon.

During these same years, the Canadian and Australian experiences were being assessed in articles appearing in the *Nuova Antologia* which maintained the usefulness of the deportation or forced emigration of undesirable elements or of excess population. Changes in the relations between Great Britain and her colonies were also studied in order to assess the benefits which Italy might gain from a similar emigration policy.[10] Fragmentary and marginal, but nevertheless continuous, information on Canada's growth added to this theoretical debate. The *Politecnico*, for example, constantly published data on the construction of new stretches of railway and bridges in Canada, while the *Annali Universali di Statistica* provided information on British, Irish and Northern European emigration to the Dominion. Even if relatively little was being printed about Canada in Italian newspapers, a great deal of foreign and Canadian material was nevertheless being read and acquired: from history texts and government pamphlets on British immigration to Canada, to monographs on education, agriculture, and the mining industry in various provinces.

In these years, Enea Cavalieri published an account of his 1876 trip to the United States and Canada which initially appeared as a series of articles for the *Nuova Antologia*, and subsequently as a book.[11] Cavalieri was a thinker who had studied a wide variety of issues and had among other things contributed to the famous inquiry by Sidney Sonnino and Leopoldo Franchetti on the social, economic, and administrative situation in Sicily and to other investigations on the condition of the Italian South. This background makes the account of his Canadian trip particularly interesting. On his travels, he was an attentive observer of the conditions of Italian immigrants and more generally of the immigration policy of the countries which he visited.

In his North American trip, Cavalieri went first to Canada even though he knew that "in leaving Europe, rarely does one go anywhere other than to the United States.'' In his opinion, however,

> the Provinces of Canada deserved a more careful visit because the colonial ties which existed there brought old Europe in contact with young America, and thus offered an interesting opportunity for comparison and study.[12]

In this context, he dedicated a large part of his trip and his subsequent articles to Canadian institutions, to the economy of the country, and to its relations with Europe, especially England. Cavalieri carried letters of introduction which allowed him to meet Canadians who guided him during his visits to the various provinces.

As might be expected, the author took note of the number of Italian immigrants living in every city and province he visited; however, in contrast to his comments on the United States, he wrote very little about the Italian immigrant experience in Canada. His only remark was that ''they had been sent there for family reasons more than by choice; the community included a number of music teachers, marble-cutters, figurine-makers and other profit seekers.''[13]

What most interested him about immigration to Canada were the programmes and conditions of assisted immigration which seemed to him to be motivated particularly by philanthropic and humanitarian factors. Immigration officers seemed very different from the profiteers who attracted European workers to the United States.

> What is most surprising and makes one truly think that emigration officers must after all be acting from

> sincere conviction, is the skillfulness with which they give their work the appearance and motivation of a philanthropic mission or of an effort to improve the social order.[14]

Cavalieri was particularly fascinated by the promotion of child immigration from England:

> I wonder whether we should not also be promoting a similar programme of child emigration from the Neapolitan provinces, rather than allowing them to be sold to profiteers who subject them to all manner of tyranny and ill-treatment.[15]

Like most liberals and Italian Catholics, Cavalieri placed great trust in public and private institutions whose function it was to help the poor and the emigrants. It did not occur to him that the State and charitable institutions were practising on a greater scale the same *commercio di carne umana* of which the *padroni* and non-governmental emigration agents were accused. Historian Robert Harney deserves recognition among other things for having challenged the stereotype of the *padrone* as an exploiter and speculator.[16] Harney emphasized the extent to which this person answered the migrant's needs for work and other basic necessities. While it is obvious that the *padrone* speculated on the immigrants' work, he was providing them, indeed selling them, the services of a go-between which they could later forego when they acquired sufficient knowledge of the host country, formed mutual aid societies, or joined trade unions. The immigrant aid or charitable societies which Cavalieri so admired, on the contrary, sought to play a pre-eminent role within the local Italian communities, above all because they had been legitimated by the Italian government and also because they represented the values and the elite of the country of origin. Cavalieri tended to minimize the criticisms directed against the activities of the Italian consulates in North America and against the local elites of the immigrant communities.[17] He was favourably disposed toward schemes of Italian immigration to Canada.

He especially valued those schemes which entailed government control of Italian emigration because the emigrant would no longer be left to his own devices: the poor man would be protected and guided by those more capable of deciding his future. It was this paternalistic point of view which differentiated Italian intellectuals from the Italo-American elites in their relations with the poor immigrant. For the former, the poor immigrant was considered part of the human landscape of contemporary Italy: it was necessary to protect him and ensure that his misery would turn into dignified poverty. For the latter, of which New York mayor Fiorello LaGuardia was a noteworthy example, the poor Italian immigrant, specifically the organ-grinder, represented a past to be forgotten and buried. LaGuardia therefore forbade street musicians from entering his city.

The tolerant and protective attitude towards the Italian immigrant so characteristic of Cavalieri was also to be found in Italian writings on emigration. Although these writings preferred the respectable emigrant to the street musician, they nevertheless acknowledged that in some way even the street musician represented Italy. When the commentator of the Paris exhibition of 1878 saw the painting by Conick depicting the female street musician, he observed:

> Not one Italian landscape at foreign exhibitions is without its piper or gypsy... but in Conick's case we cannot be angry. Her large black eyes look at the beholder with an expression of such pure innocence as to inspire a deep sense of pity for this vagabond. The picturesque costume with its lively colours adds a sense of fascination to the aura of melancholy which her face exudes. She resembles a Mignon who amidst dark northern fogs thinks of her country with its clear blue sky where warm and perfumed breezes blow and where golden orange trees blossom.[18]

It was in this spirit of paternalistic tolerance and condescension that the first biographies of Italians abroad were written at the end of the nineteenth century. From the biographies and bibliographies of explorers, missionaries, travellers, and adventurers, emigration began to be seen as a centuries-old phenomenon in a country that could not offer good work opportunities or a decent life to its inhabitants. Many of these biographies and first dictionaries of Italians abroad[19] were devoid of that rhetoric of *italianità*, of those hagiographic tendencies, which were so characteristic of nationalist writings at the beginning of the century and later during fascism.

Although these early works were crude and imprecise, they did express a new approach to the phenomenon of emigration considered to be a structural fact which had somehow created a link between Italy and the world. Naturally these biographies were also devised to make Italian communities abroad appear respectable and to instill in them a sense of cultural and historical affinity with the country of origin, although these themes were not as pronounced as in later writings.

These studies and public discussions were not followed up by legislative action to protect the emigrants. The law of 1888 sought above all to control their numbers by regulating the issuance of passports and to require the registration of emigration agencies. These agencies were thereby made liable in two ways: they had to pledge a security, which in fact was a minimal amount that could be subdivided among a large number of associates who thus acquired the right to name an indefinite number of subagents; the agencies were required as well to provide the emigrant with a contract, but could do so at the moment of embarkment when he would have had no time to report a fraud without literally missing the boat.

Overall, the growth of emigration from the British Isles and Northern Europe to Canada stimulated a theoretical discussion in Italy on the models of European colonization of the New World. However, the Italian government did not learn how to direct this migratory flow from its shores to foreign countries. It dealt with the experience of emigrants only after the fact, that is, only when permanent emigration became a concrete reality or when temporary emigration to a particular country became so widespread as to warrant a fact-finding inquiry.

These studies of emigration were carried on in the context of dreams of conquest of new territories. From the end of the nineteenth century, Italian exhibitions generally had a section on Italians abroad, on Italian colonies, and on missionary work, which were meant ideally to represent Italian expansion beyond its borders. The failure of colonial enterprises meant that an always greater importance was attached to the development of "colonies of infiltration," that is, areas of large Italian immigration, as if even in this way Italy was extending its influence abroad.

At the same time, Italian consuls sent home reports on emigrants, on their progress, on their failures, on the future prospects of Little Italies. In the *Bolletino del Ministero degli Affari Esteri*, a report was published in 1901 by the Consul General in Montreal, Giuseppe Solimbergo, entitled "An Economic and Political View of Canada." It began with a general description of the country, included opinions on the settlement of the provinces, and ended with an analysis of the situation of Italian immigrants and their future prospects.[20]

The Consul provided a negative assessment of the agricultural settlement of the Northwest. The Canadian government bore "the direct and real costs of enlisting and transporting various loads of emigrants from the most disparate and heterogeneous races: Mennonites, Galician Austrians, Croatians, Armenians, Rumanians, Finns, Doukhobors, etc."[21] Indeed, according to Solimbergo, this government initiative had failed because these "strange settlers" after having received so much help, were incapable of confronting setbacks and turned to the "milder climes of the American Pacific." The results of a project, supported by the Canadian clergy, to repatriate French-Canadian emigrants who had settled in the United States were considered to be just as negative.

In Solimbergo's opinion, this was due to the problems of agricultural settlement in Canada, which required a large amount of initial capital to overcome the inevitable calamities of the early years. One was led to conclude that Canadian projects of agricultural settlement as they were promoted in Italy could only be undertaken by people with sufficient capital to withstand the heavy costs of first settlement. If this were the case and the enterprise could also attract "poor Italian working class families according to the conditions set down by the law,'' it might produce good profits for rich Italian settlers since the high cost of local labour would be avoided.[22] In the present situation, Solimbergo reported, ''there is heavier emigration from Northern Italy to South America'' where emigrants tended to maintain their agricultural pursuits, whereas Canada largely attracted Italians from the South who looked for work in the cities and often changed jobs.

> [In addition to the construction of railways and canals] they find jobs as small travelling vendors of fruit, milk, or heating oil; in industrial establishments relating to cotton and iron; in the production of bricks and tiles; in sawmills or in mineral quarries closest to urban centres; in urban building projects, particularly in snow removal; in the manufacture and distribution of plaster and wood statuettes; in stone and marble works for cemeteries; in railway stations and dock work, etc. Very few have been able to establish a small drygoods store with items imported or made in Italy, with a boarding house, with a bar to sell beer and spirits; a few have gone into market gardening with a fair degree of success.... Very few have reached a fairly good social standing and they have done so by widening their own business interests slowly but surely so as to obtain a share in the public works projects of smaller cities.[23]

Despite the consulate's requests, these immigrants in fact only got in touch with it either to settle their military status, to obtain birth, marriage or death certificates, or notarial documents, to deal with work grievances, or for personal reasons. The consulate had therefore been unable to establish relations with all the immigrants. Only with great difficulty did it succeed in compiling a fairly complete register of Italians resident in Montreal and in getting an approximate picture of the distribution of Italians in Canada.

Apart from the permanent nucleus of the Montreal community, there was a variable but considerable number of Italian seasonal labourers from the United States. According to Solimbergo, the majority of these rural immigrants were on the whole "intensely good," but "those elements that little by little rise out of and dominate this group (I would like to say the intellectually superior product of this mass of people) is in many respects considerably inferior to the average from the standpoint of morality."[24] The Consul despised "the recruiters and hoarders of men and work, speculators and intermediaries of every kind,"[25] who had obtained influence over this mass of immigrants through their entrepreneurial skills.

Like Cavalieri, the Consul General was in other words distinguishing between "the successful, the notables, those who after a long stay in the country managed to build a decent fortune and a family"[26] and the labour brokers, the operators of boarding houses and other services for temporary immigrants. This distinction arose from the desire of the consul, of bureaucrats in general, and of the Italian notables in Canada as elsewhere, to alter the organization and division of social roles which had emerged during the sojourning phase. They wanted to remove the *padrone*'s prestige and influence and to favour the representatives of legitimate authority and the traditional Italian elite. Since Italian workers abroad did not contact their consulates because intermediaries and bosses provided the services they needed, Solimbergo believed that only by subverting their power could the Italian authorities reacquire status within the Italian community and the larger society. This is a process well described by Robert Harney and analyzed by Bruno Ramirez in his book, *Les Premiers Italiens de Montréal*.[27]

It is possible that Solimbergo even considered Italo-Canadian entrepreneurs a potential means for increasing trade between Canada and Italy, as we shall see below. Analyzing the value of exports and imports between the two countries from 1878 onwards, Solimbergo arrived at the conclusion that there was a constant and significant increase, despite the fact that a large part of both countries' products travelled on foreign ships. Once again, the problem first outlined by Cristoforo Negri confronted the Consul. It concerned the encouragement of direct trade relations between Canada and Italy and the use of local Italian initiative to develop more lasting links with Canadian businessmen.

Solimbergo studied various methods of promoting direct commercial links such as Italy sending commercial agents or representatives of individual firms to Canada or the establishment of a permanent commercial agency in the country. He personally favoured the latter option because it meant that Italy would be "represented on the spot by a permanent agent who would be well-known and respected in local commercial circles and whose name alone would provide the best of guarantees."[28] The Consul was probably thinking here of some Italo-Canadian entrepreneur who could follow the example of German immigration by promoting trade between the country of origin and that of settlement. Solimbergo summarized the latter's experience in the following terms:

> Even though there are few Germans in Canada they have a lot of capital and enterprise. They are mindful of their far distant homeland and are attached to it, visiting it almost every year. They almost consider themselves their country's natural commercial representatives and try to link as many of their interests as possible to it.[29]

As with other students of immigration, Solimbergo had understood one of the consequences of the immigrants' experience. Their presence helped to make known the products of their country of origin and to introduce new culinary and aesthetic tastes. As Harney has observed, it was the fruit vendors, figurine-makers, marble cutters, and travelling musicians, more than the travelling salesmen or promotional agents, who created a need for goods previously unknown or at first considered totally foreign to the culture or tastes of the host country.[30] Solimbergo and others, however, did not realize one of the side effects of the immigrants' activity: they created over time small and large businesses which produced Italian goods in the host country itself, thereby reducing the existing market for imported goods. This was a phenomenon of which Cavalieri had noted the origins when he visited the United States. A similar process was taking place at the beginning of the century in Canada. Italo-Canadian businessmen were creating enterprises which produced food, building materials, furniture, and musical instruments which, in part, satisfied the demand for Italian products. The notables and *prominenti* of the Little Italies were interested in improving the image of the Italian community of Canada both to gain prestige and appointments from the Canadian government and recognition and legitimation from Italy.

For these reasons, the Italo-Canadian elite felt threatened by the negative publicity arising from a series of articles published in Milan's *Corriere della Sera* between February and June of 1901 on the misfortunes of Italian immigrants in Canada. These articles had even given rise to a parliamentary debate in Italy. The elite's reaction was two-fold: on the one hand, they increased their contributions for the building of schools, churches, orphanages, and homes to show that they wanted to reinforce the cohesion of the Little Italies and to assist poor immigrants; on the other, they promoted lectures and articles in Italy designed to present the mishaps described in the *Corriere* as isolated incidents occasioned more by the immigrants' ignorance and inexperience than the Canadian employers' ill-will.[31]

The Italo-Canadian notables were trying to make the point that if the "business of immigration" were entrusted to worthy and respectable people and to immigrant aid societies, they would not have allowed immigrants to have been abandoned after their arrival in Canada. Instead, they would have prevented the immigration of people who did not have the financial or occupational resources required by the host country.

Even the Canadian government which, as is well known, was opposed to Southern Italian immigrants because of their poverty and strange customs, felt obliged to re-establish in Italy its image as a well organized and welcoming country, willing to receive and help those qualified to come. For this reason, Canada participated in the International Exhibition held in 1906 (though it had been scheduled for 1904) in Milan to inaugurate the Sempione railway tunnel. The Canadian pavilion, which cost 250,000 Italian lira was designed to highlight the natural resources of the country.

> The impression one gets upon entering the building is that of a pagan temple dedicated to the god of plenty. A large hall the size of an immense nave is decorated in an original fashion with heavily laden ears of wheat, animals' heads, and paintings of a variety of fruit arranged so as to stand out on a red background which is the basic feature of the whole setting.[32]

The image of Canada presented at the exhibition resembled seventeenth-century descriptions of New France as a land of spontaneous generation which promised easy yields and which hid enormous mineral wealth. An idyllic picture was offered of a harmonious and prosperous life.

The obvious intent of the exhibition was to stimulate Italian immigration to Canada and, in fact, one thousand or so requests were received by the committee which was charged with collecting the names of prospective emigrants. It has not been possible to verify, however, if these requests were actually accepted. Nevertheless, this propaganda was successful, among other things because those who attended Milan's exhibition traditionally came from the countryside and they found attractive the image presented of Canada as a paradise near at hand. An Italian observer remarked:

> The dream of a small plot of land, rich and fertile, is evocative but hides the sacrifices which the land demands of the settler before it may yield him, let us say for the sake of argument, a hundredfold. In any case the pavilion is one of the ones most visited and the brochure on Canada which depicts the country in rosy hues is distributed by the thousands in our area.

> The peasant who comes back from the Exhibition, his head dizzy and swollen then quietly reads and reflects on the pamphlet. And often the result is that he requests from the Commissioner those sixty-four hectares which are supposed to bring him happiness.[33]

The monograph distributed during the exhibition was entitled *Canada and the New Century: Nine Provinces of the Last Best West*, edited by Sidney Fisher, Minister of Agriculture. Its purpose was to explain "Canada's display, its products, land, laws, liberty, order, happiness, prosperity, and general invitation to industrious people." This pamphlet was accompanied by another, *Twentieth-Century Canada with an Atlas of Western Canada for the Prospective Settler.*[34] The Canadian exhibit and the two pamphlets were clearly intended to refute the negative impression of the life of Italian immigrants and to minimize the difficulties which potential immigrants might experience if they wanted to settle in Canada as farmers.

For its part the Italian government did not actively aid those who wished to emigrate. It preferred to delegate this responsibility to the Italian Immigrant Aid Society for Canada which enjoyed its full support. This support was obvious in the composition of its board of directors: the honorary president was the Consul General, Count Mazza, and the president, C.H. Catelli, was an important businessman and son of a former Italian consul. Other officials included the industrialist, Casimiro Mariotti, the lawyer, Gerolamo Internoscia, the pastor of the Italian parish, and the editor of *La Patria Italiana.*[35] Established by twenty-five individuals who all contributed to a start-up fund, the organization was intended, "to assist and encourage Italian emigrants to come to Canada and insofar as funds permit, to lend money to those who would wish to settle on the land and who are considered a desirable class of immigrant.''[36] The Society was expected to contact the federal and provincial governments in order to obtain lots of land suited to the needs of Italian farmers and to persuade the local authorities to have Italian-speaking agents in these areas. If the Society were unable to secure such agents, it would hire men to perform this task under its immediate control.[37]

Financially, the Society expected that contributions from private and public institutions, as well as the fee charged to the immigrant for services rendered, would augment the start up fund originally subscribed by the founding members.[38] It also counted on ''the cooperation of the Banco di Napoli to protect deposits and financial transactions.''[39] In other words, the Society intended to institute a large-scale process of mediation between Italian labourers, the Italian and Canadian governments, the provincial governments, and local employers in order to transform Italian immigrants into agricultural settlers. The fact is, however, that the Society did not seriously intend to direct potential settlers to agricultural jobs.

> Most often it is important to find profitable work which permits easy savings, while getting used to the climate, the environment, and to new methods of land cultivation, learning a little of the language, and refining oneself in order to appear more *acceptable*: these are our Society's aims.[40]

In short, this was an organization which, under the guise of patriotism and humanitarianism, used the methods of the emigration agents and *padroni* (such as the extension of loans, the collection of fees for services rendered, and mediation between employers and workers).

The Italian government continued above all to be interested in reaching a trade accord with Canada. This was made abundantly clear when it entrusted Marco Doria with a fact-finding inquiry on Canada in 1905-1906, and did not even bother to ask him for a report on Italian immigration to that country.[41] Doria believed that an improvement of bilateral trade would facilitate Italian settlement in Canada, even though he did not take the trouble to show the relationship between the one and the other. On the basis of documents thus far available, the link in Doria's mind, as in Solimbergo's before him, appears to have been the Italian Immigrant Aid Society. But Canada was especially seen as an important producer of natural resources and as a potential market for Italian goods. As Doria observed:

> We must not only look upon Canada as a hospitable land which will welcome a large part of our emigrants, while respecting their language and culture, but also as a market to be captured, as a place from which to acquire the natural resources that we need.[42]

Doria's appeal largely remained a dead letter. On the road to bilateral trade relations, the Italian government took such small steps that the 1909 negotiations on a trade agreement fell through and Canada worked out an accord with France instead. Only in the following year when Italy threatened to retaliate against Canadian imports did the Canadian Finance Minister conclude a temporary tariff agreement on a list of specific items with the Consul General, Lionello Scelsi. Other imports were subject to the existing import duties if they arrived in Canada indirectly.[43]

Between the late nineteenth and early twentieth centuries, the image of Canada as a more orderly society than the United States became more pronounced in Italy. The country's development was seen as a slow evolution from colony to nation, even though its links with the mother country remained strong. According to the above mentioned Italian writers, immigration to Canada was aided by the federal and provincial governments to a greater extent than in the United States which left too much to individual initiative, whether the results be personal success or failure. According to this view, Canada respected the language and cultural rights of French Canadians as well as the ethnic settlements of Germans, Mennonites and Doukhobors, and the assumption was that as much would be done for Italians.

But the immigrant rarely was the central focus of these writers' attention. They saw him instead as a means by which Italy could attain a desired objective, be it economic and political expansion in the world or the solution to serious demographic and developmental problems. In this context, the immigrant was perceived as helpless and therefore in need of the notables' assistance so that his grinding poverty could be turned into dignified indigence. The notables for their part considered him an embarrassment and they believed that by eliminating the nefarious influence of *padroni* and other middlemen, they would make him more *civile* and less *cafone*. In this way, their own position in Canadian society would be augmented. No one it seems saw the immigrant from his own perspective or in his real context, with his needs, strategies, and objectives or with his problems of work, housing, and integration into Canadian life.

Just as with the aborted trade agreement, the Italian government failed to play an active role in helping the immigrant settle in the new land. It was in this period that the presence in Canada of Italian immigrants underwent a radical change. Those who had arrived in the country intending to stay temporarily, came to reinforce the permanent urban nuclei of the emerging Little Italies. This process was supported by the traditional forms of family and *paese* networks, in which the Italian government and the local elite did not play an active role. It is not surprising that on the eve of the Great War, Professor Carlo De Stefani, addressing the Georgic Academy of Florence on the topic "Canada and Italian emigration" once again bemoaned, in the same tones of condescension toward the immigrant and of national self-interest, the lack of public awareness and the inertia of the Italian government:

> Canada deserves to be much better known to us, rich and poor alike. To facilitate this periodic and temporary or permanent process of emigration which is so useful to us and to Canada, to exploit this newly opened field, requires that the government and the consuls (who are too few and poorly equipped) act wisely. This means the elimination or strict surveillance of emigration agents to insure that they do not pocket a good portion of the workers' salaries. The reputation of Italians, as seen through the worst elements which have made their way to the United States and through others who are intelligent, but poorly educated and fomenters of strikes, is held in poor regard and is no better than that of the Blacks. The esteem and the prominence of citizens are in keeping

with the energy and the strength of the State to which they belong.[44]

NOTES

1. See Piero Del Negro, *Il Canada nella cultura veneziana del Settecento*, in Luca Codignola, ed., *Canadiana. Storia e Storiografia canadese* (Venice, 1979), 47-66; Piero Del Negro, *Per una bibliografia italo-canadese. Il Canada nella pubblicistica italiana dell'età moderna* in Luca Codignola ed., *Canadiana. Problemi di storia canadese* (Venice, 1983), 13-31.

2. Cristoforo Negri, "Le navigazioni alla Nuova-Brunswick," in *La Grandezza Italiana. Studi, confronti, desideri* (Turin, 1864), 109. The article first appeared in the Turin daily *Monarchia Nazionale*, September 2, 1863.

3. *Ibid.*, 110.

4. *Ibid.*, 109.

5. The publication of the *Bolletino Consolare*, begun in Turin in 1862, continued in Florence and then in Rome under the new title *Bolletino del Ministero degli Affari Esteri.*

6. Negri, *La Grandezza*, 8.

7. *Ibid.*, 149-150.

8. *Ibid.*, 154.

9. Leone Carpi, *Dell'emigrazione italiana all'estero nei suoi rapporti coll'agricoltura, coll'industria e col commercio* (Florence, 1871).

10. See for example Giovanni Branchi, "Il sistema coloniale studiato da un italiano in Australia," *Nuova Antologia* IV (1872), 147-69; G. Emilia Cerruti, "Le colonie penali e le colonie libere," *ibid.*, II (1873), 673-722; Girolamo Boccardo, "L'emigrazione e le colonie," *ibid.*, I (1874), 621-50.

11. See Enea Cavalieri, "Il dominion del Canada. Appunti di Viaggio," *Nuova Antologia*, February 16, March 16, April 16, 1879; also published as a book entitled *In giro per il mondo. Osservazioni e appunti* (Bologna, 1880).

12. Cavalieri, *In giro*, 3.

13. *Ibid.*, 89. According to Cavalieri the 1870 Canadian Census registered 1,035 residents of Italian nationality born in Italy. Of these, 414 resided in cities (191 in Montreal, 34 in Toronto).

14. *Ibid.*, 134.

15. *Ibid.*, 101.

16. Robert F. Harney, "The Padrone and the Immigrant," *Canadian Review of American Studies* 5 (1974), 101-18.

17. Cavalieri attributed criticism against De Luca, Consul of New York, the anticlerical demonstrations during the inauguration of the Columbus monument in Philadelphia, and other episodes of internal tension in the Italian community of the United States to purely factious politics. In addition, for example, he maintained that the entire New York Italian community was working against the trade in immigrant children when the Italian publication *Libertà e Associazione* of Milan, reporting on the activities of the

Piedmontese traveller and publicist, Cesare Celso Moreno, regarding the protection of children stated that the Italian community accused Moreno of fanaticism and of giving Italians a bad reputation. According to the publication "he [Moreno] did the work *that the Italian Minister in Washington and the consuls were paid to do and should have done*" ("Gli Schiavi Italiani negli Stati Uniti," *Libertà e Associazone*, August 9, 1874).

18. *L'Esposizione di Parigi del 1878 illustrata* II (Milano, 1879), 607-08.

19. See for example Francesco Fortunato Carloni, *Gli Italiani all'estero* (Città di Castello, 1890); Leo Benvenuti, *Dizionario degli italiani all'estero* (Florence, 1890).

20. "Il Canadà sotto l'aspetto economico e politico. Rapporto del Comm. Giuseppe Solimbergo, R. Console Generale in Montreal" *Bollettino del Ministero degli Affari Esteri*, no. 190 (March 1901), 169-205; G. Solimbergo, *ibid.*, "Emigrazione al Canadà", 277-278.

21. *Ibid.*, 183.

22. *Ibid.*, 185-86.

23. *Ibid.*, 203.

24. *Ibid.*, 205.

25. *Ibid.*

26. *Ibid.*, 203.

27. See Robert Harney, *Dalla Frontiera alle Little Italies* (Rome, 1984) and Bruno Ramirez, *Les premiers Italiens de Montréal. L'origine de la Petite Italie du Québec* (Montréal, 1984).

28. Solimbergo, "Il Canadà sotto l'aspetto," 193.

29. *Ibid.*, 189.

30. Robert Harney, "L'immigrazione italiana e le frontiere della civiltà occidentale," *Dalla Frontiera*, 39-72.

31. See for example Domenico Rebecca's correspondence from Montreal "Lettere dal Canadà," "*L'Esplorazione Commerciale. Giornale di viaggi e di geografia commerciale* (1901), 273-76. He was sent by the Treviso Committee for the Protection of Emigrants. Commenting on the facts narrated in the *Corriere della Sera*, he said that "Canada is certainly not the place nor is any other country for that matter for unsettled people, without education, without solid backing, good for simply ordinary occupations." (*ibid.*, 273).

32. "Il padiglione del Canadà," *Esposizione di Milano 1906* V (Milan, October 30, 1906), 146.

33. *Ibid.*

34. Such pamphlets, both printed in Ottawa in 1906, had been published in French and English.

35. The data and quotations that follow are taken from the book by the clergyman Pietro Pisani, *Il Canada presente e futuro in relazione all'emigrazione italiana* (Rome, 1909) written following a study trip in Canada. Pisani, who dealt for many years with Italian emigration according to the views of the Bishop of Cremona, Bonomelli, wrote

again about Italian emigration in Canada in "L'emigrazione italiana nell'America del Nord. Note e proposte," *Rivista Internazionale* (1911).

36. *Ibid.*, 37, article 16 from the Constitution of Italian Immigrant Aid Society for Canada.

37. *Ibid.*, 36.

38. *Ibid.*

39. *Ibid.*, 37, articles 17-32 of the same constitution.

40. *Ibid.*, 37.

41. Letter from Marco Doria-Lamba to Pietro Pisani, Genoa, March 13, 1909, published by Pisani, *Il Canada presente*, 171.

42. *Ibid.*, 167.

43. See Canada, Department of External Affairs, *Documents on Canadian External Relations* I (Ottawa 1967-1980), 728-32.

44. Carlo De Stefani, *Il Canada e l'emigrazione italiana* (Firenze, 1914), 12-13.

Workers Without a Cause: Italian Immigrant Labour in Montreal, 1880-1930

Bruno Ramirez

The early years of this century were a period of massive immigration to Canada and of sweeping changes in regional and local labour markets. This context makes it particularly interesting to reconstruct the work experience of Italian immigrants who joined the Canadian labour market in large numbers precisely at that moment.

The Canadian hinterland was one of the poles of immigrant labour. Jobs in railroad construction, mining, lumbering, and harvesting were essentially seasonal in character and followed closely the evolution of industrial geography both at a regional and national level. It was this segment of the labour market that first attracted the largest quantity of Italian workers, giving rise to such phenomena as sojourning and *padronismo* so well studied by Robert Harney and Donald Avery among others.[1]

The focus here, however, will be on the Canadian city

and specifically on Montreal. The urban immigrant labour market was acquiring its own distinctive features in this period and would soon become an integral part of Montreal's economy. This aspect of the labour market has received little systematic treatment. But its importance should not be underestimated since it allows us to place the work experience of Italian immigrants at the centre of the process of settlement.

At the same time, it is important to see the interaction between the metropolitan and hinterland labour markets and the temporal links connecting them. If at first they seem to follow two separate courses, their interrelation becomes clearer toward the end of the nineteenth century. As migrants increasingly were recruited through Montreal's employment agencies, they came in contact, however briefly, with the structures of the city's existing Italian community.[2] They consequently learned about job possibilities within the urban economy. Later on, migrants were drawn to Montreal by the possibility of reconstituting kinship and hometown networks. Of course, these developments would not have been possible without the growing demand for an urban-based unskilled labour force. This demand, it seems, originated primarily from two sectors of the Montreal economy: large-scale commercial services and utilities; and the construction of urban infrastructures.

Because Montreal was at the centre of a regional and continental transportation network, it had a variety of facilities which were essential for servicing the transportation industry: a harbour, railway stations, junctions, depots, freight yards among others. Each of these required, although in differing degrees, a pool of labour primarily for loading and unloading, and for other unskilled work.

As early as 1895, Italian labourers were reported as working on the docks of the harbour.[3] It was, however, the railroad facilities which generated the largest demand for day labourers. Besides the two downtown stations, Bonaventure and Windsor, the Canadian Pacific and the Grand Trunk had a number of sites throughout the metropolitan area and surroundings, ranging from the Angus shops where locomotives were produced and repaired to simple railway junctions, at Côte St-Luc for instance. In most of these work sites, general labour could either be hired to fill temporary demands or, less frequently, to fill permanent positions.

In addition, the Montreal Street Railway Company (MSRC) through its various facilities, absorbed an important contingent of Italian labourers. Besides providing work in its maintenance shops and depots, this company generated a lot of work in the laying and maintenance of tracks. Here too, much of the hiring was cyclical: rising during the summer months and ending with the start of the cold season. As early as the summer of 1904, the MSRC employed about 300 Italian labourers; but of these, less than a third were kept in the company's employ during the ensuing winter. The latter were used mostly for shovelling snow.[4] In subsequent years, as the street railway network expanded considerably, the MSRC became one of the major employers of Italians. Among the utility companies, probably the largest employer of Italian labourers was the Monreal Light, Heat and Power Company (MLHP). In 1904, roughly one hundred of the 250 or so labourers in its employ were Italians.[5]

The second sector of the Montreal labour market absorbing a significant contingent of Italian labourers involved the building of urban infrastructures such as canals, sewers, tunnels, streets, as well as large construction projects. Here too, the demand for labour grew progressively with the expansion and modernization of the city and here too, in fact more so than in the previous sector, employment was seasonal, ranging from a few days to an entire season. One source recalled that in order to obtain work in this sector, workers had to be at the hiring site every morning and wait in line. "You had to stay there and just wait; and if they didn't take you, you had to come back the next day."[6] In many of the large construction projects, work was organized in gangs. Vincenzo Monaco, who laboured as a canal builder in Montreal's East End, stated that excavation work was done by gangs of two to three hundred workers. "Since many of us were Italians, there sometimes was an interpreter who directed our work."[7]

It is impossible to reconstruct the seasonal fluctuations of this sector of the urban labour market, but its capacity to absorb large amounts of immigrant labour is beyond question. In 1904, for instance, when the fraudulent advertising of two local "padroni" resulted in an over-supply of Italian labourers in the city, the MLHP Company took advantage of the bonanza of cheap labour to hire a number of them. As a company representative explained, "... we happened to be falling over them in the streets. Then we thought we might as well get all the work done we could while there was such a large influx of men."[8] In 1912, the CPR began to construct a tunnel under Mount Royal. The demand for labourers was so large that some had to be imported from the United States.[9] In the same year, employers voiced concern that the outbreak of the Balkan conflict would result in a critical shortage of labour in Montreal since immigrants from those areas were returning home.

As long as immigration from Italy persisted, the hinterland and urban labour markets continued to exist, although the latter was becoming more attractive to Italian immigrants. In fact, the relative importance of the two markets, both in terms of their absorptive capacity and of the immigrants' own preference, became reversed. A study of the La Tuque mining area done in 1910 by an Italian immigration inspector found that out of 3,500 workers employed by the MacDonald and O'Brien Company 1,000 were Italians. The author pointed out that the company would have hired more Italians if it had been able to find them. The problem was in fact the attraction that Montreal exerted on immigrant labour. City wages had become higher than what could be earned at La Tuque. The author concluded that most of the Italian immigrants working in that northern Quebec location were *novizi*, recently arrived, ignorant of the local labour market, and easily recruited by labour agencies.[10] Similarly, when Nicola Manzo first came to Montreal in 1911, the first job he could get was through a *padrone* who sent him to a railway construction site in Ontario with a gang of labourers. But when the season ended, he returned to settle in the city.[11] Costanzo D'Amico, on the other hand, arrived in Montreal with his brother, intending to go to Sault Ste. Marie where an uncle was working. But the two soon changed their mind: "We decided to remain here because several of our *paesani* who lived here explained to us that Montreal was a better place to live."[12]

The emergence of a number of Italian neighbourhoods in Montreal and the cultural and psychological effects that this *ambiente* had on newcomers will not be dealt with here. Still it is interesting to note that by the second decade of the century, this process was well under way. By then two parishes and a score of associations had been established and kinship and *paesi* networks were being reconstituted. To the immigrant, Montreal no longer appeared as an urban frontier trapping him in some cold slum for a long winter or sending him off to some remote corner of the Canadian West. Instead it had become a place where he could both work and live, shop in his own language, celebrate with friends and relatives his *paese*'s patron saint, and where he was more and more likely to find a wife and raise a family.

This last point should not be underestimated. The emergence of a marriage market was a strong factor in keeping the large number of young males within the community, as well as in drawing new immigrants to the city. The parish census of 1905 listed 235 families who had already produced a sizeable group of young unmarried women. Sylvie Taschereau's study of marriages performed in Montreal's two Italian parishes from 1905 to 1930 found that a high percentage of wives were born in Quebec of Italian parents, while their husbands were born in Italy.[13] In addition, grooms on average tended to be considerably older than their brides.[14] Statistically the task of finding a wife within the Italian community was not becoming easier as time passed since the supply of young unmarried males born in Quebec from Italian parents was also rising; but at least it was now becoming possible for the immigrant to compete for one. And the best way to achieve success in this regard was for the Italian male to live in close proximity to the community. This allowed him to enter a social network which facilitated courtship and marriage.

There was a more basic reason for the Italian immigrant's growing attraction to the city, and that was his fear of the hostility that he might encounter in remote, far away work sites where one's life and daily existence were ultimately in the hands of some boss or company owner and where even the simplest legal recourse was outside the realm of his possibilities. Italians living in Quebec must have been shocked by the news that three of their countrymen working in the interior on the construction of a canal had been beaten up without provocation by local people and that one of them had died from his injuries.[15] More shocking still was the leniency shown by the court who let the accused men off with incredibly light sentences. Stories of mistreatment and abuses in remote work sites seemed to circulate rapidly among the city's Italian population. In 1904 an Italian worker told the reporter of a Montreal daily that, "il Sig. Giuseppe is the most popular person within our colony."[16] He was referring to Giuseppe Maffei, a foreman with an Italian gang on a Manitoba construction site, who had heroically defended his countrymen against the abuses of some Canadian foremen. It was a story of pride and honour recounted in detail by the newspaper with Maffei's picture at the centre of the page. But it was one of those happy stories which among the city's Italian population stood as a reminder of the harshness of the working life in those Godforsaken places.

Of course working and living in the city did not exempt Italian immigrants from harsh treatment and discrimination. In fact the record shows that the chances of conflict with the local native population were even greater because, of all major North American cities, Montreal saw the most intense competition between native and immigrant workers. This consideration should be central to any study of social conflict and crime among the Italian population of the city. The nascent Italian community was by no means a harmonious micro-universe free from internal conflict and even violence. But when Italians felt they were the victims of group discrimination and mistreatment, the possibility for mobilizing the community existed. As early as 1895, after a brawl had erupted between Italian and Canadian dockworkers in Montreal, the Italians held a public meeting during which their specific work situation became a community issue. But equally interesting, the Canadians involved in the dispute brought their grievances to Italian community leaders hoping that they might influence the Italian workers.[17] It would appear then that Italian workers already were perceived in Montreal labour circles not simply as wage-earners, but also as a collective entity precisely defined by bonds of nationality.

Undoubtedly the most important expression of ethnic solidarity during that initial stage of settlement was the Giaccone affair.[18] In 1904, Giuseppe Giaccone, a tailor well known to the community for having resided in the city for almost 10 years, shot and killed a French Canadian who was trying to beat him up. This affair soon became a *cause célèbre* when the court handed down a death sentence by hanging. Not only were the Italians convinced that Giaccone had fired in self-defence, they felt humiliated because the verdict stated explicity that the particularly heavy sentence was meant as an example to deter foreigners from committing acts of violence.

There was an immediate mobilization to save Giaccone's life. Money was raised to help with legal costs; petitions were sent to all levels of government, including the King; and the Italian connection was also used to obtain the Pope's intervention. Finally the day before the execution, news arrived that the sentence had been commuted to life imprisonment. Clearly, the community had intervened to preserve its own public image and honour, but in the process it had shown that it could save the life of one of its members.

The attraction that the urban labour market exerted on Italian immigrants was therefore not only economic — the existing demand for common labourers and the Italian immigrants' ability to insert themselves in that market — but also psychic and cultural. The greater sense of protection one felt in being part of a network of social relations from which one could potentially draw solidarity and support, and the greater possibilities for participating in the socio-cultural life of the host society must have exerted a strong influence. But it should be added that these economic and cultural considerations were in fact much more interrelated than one might suppose. The sociability that the Italian immigrant helped to produce by inserting himself in the urban milieu and in a network of relationships made possible the transformation of certain non-monetary resources (family organization, kinship and hometown-based relationships, technical know-how) into economic benefits.[19]

The dynamics of labour relations prevalent in Montreal's immigrant labour market prevented Italian workers from making the workplace the base for an "emancipatory strategy."[20] As the major employer of Italian common labourers, Canadian Pacific provides excellent documentary material on which to test this statement. As was already indicated, Canadian Pacific was integrated into Montreal's metropolitan fabric with more than a dozen facilities responding to precise criteria of division of labour and operational efficiency. These facilities absorbed a considerable number of Italians from 1900 to 1930. There are, for example, fully 913 names of Italian origin in just those

Canadian Pacific employee records beginning with the letters C and D.[21] These employment statistics are currently the object of computerized study that should uncover the character and dynamics of one of the most important internal labour markets of the metropolitan region. The focus here is on a random sample of 120 cases which, despite its size, allows certain basic trends clearly to emerge.

The first concerns the distribution of Italian workers in the various facilities. A large majority of these Italians, three-quarters of them to be precise, worked at the Angus shops which of all Canadian Pacific facilities was by far the largest and no doubt ranked among the giant workplaces of Canada. Here the company manufactured locomotives and cars and this explains the extremely elaborate occupational structure found in the shops. The rest of the Italians were scattered throughout the other facilities. About two-thirds of the Italians at the Angus shops performed tasks of general labour or were classified as helpers. The remainder belonged to semi-skilled categories, and only about ten percent could be considered skilled. This reflects both the regional and occupational composition of Italian immigration to Quebec.[22]

Interestingly enough, a large majority of Italians were involved in dead-end jobs. Except for a small minority of cases, these were mostly jobs that the company opened and closed according to the productive cycle and the more general economic conditions. More striking still is the short duration of this employment and, accordingly, the high level of turn-over. Italian workers were very frequently re-hired a second time, and in some cases a third time or more. Labour relations were clearly unstable and career opportunities, extremely reduced. The ups and downs in the level of employment, however, were not exclusively determined by the company. In the majority of cases, it was the Italian labourer who took the initiative to terminate his job.

Most Italian workers were aware of the character of their employment, of its precariousness, and of the limited possibilities for advancement. The voluntary cessation of employment may also have reflected the difficulty these workers had in upgrading their skills and in obtaining jobs that would have insured their integration in the company's productive apparatus. This pattern of occupational turnover and precariousness characterized the other sectors of Italian immigrant labour (construction of urban infrastructures). What is significant here is that this unstable pattern occurred in one of the most advanced areas of Montreal's manufacturing industry. In such a situation, the immigrant had no protection, his possibilities for bargaining were nonexistent, and he moved frequently from one workplace to another following the fluctuations of the labour market. His criteria of choice of employment (when this was possible) were likely to be based not on career considerations, but primarily on pecuniary ones.

Italian immigrant workers in Montreal, therefore, became part of the peculiar dynamics of a labour market which prevented them from becoming active in the political reconstitution of the working class. While working in far from marginal sectors of the Montreal economy, they were highly segmented and spatially mobile. This situation favoured individualized exploits rather than collective action and was hardly propitious for developing an emancipatory strategy. If such a strategy existed it lay instead in the immigrant's participation in socio-economic and cultural institutions whose access had been denied him back in Italy. Here social practices could flow into collective action in order to achieve objectives which he considered legitimate and attainable (in such areas as schools, regional or mutual aid associations, and union activity), or in order to defend or protect his ethnic status in situations of conflict.

Of course, not all Italian workers remained trapped in the dynamics of the above labour market. After having zig-zagged through that market for about 10 years, Costanzo D'Amico finally managed to find permanent employment as a watchman in the Mount Royal railway tunnel. "I spent almost all my life inside that tunnel,"[23] he affirmed with a mixture of satisfaction and irony. For Vincenzo Monaco, who considered the years spent working on public construction projects as "years of slavery," the chance to get out came when he was hired by an Italian bakery. There he learned the basic rules of the small business enterprise. A few years later, despite the onset of the Depression, he was ready to risk it in the baking business in partnership with his two brothers.[24] The move from common labour to small ethnic business represents an extemely important socio-economic step. It was one of the few qualitative leaps forward for an immigrant who for whatever reason was unable to develop special skills within the industrial context. Among other things, it allowed him to invest human and psychic energies in his efforts to make a major advance toward the vision (subjective yet concrete) of economic emancipation.

Antonio Funicelli, for his part, was able to make an early break from common labour because he had learned shoemaking in his *paese*. Initially, he found a job in one of Montreal's major manufacturing enterprises, Canadian Car, but he had to perform the work of a day labourer. The following quotation reveals very clearly the contrast between his artisan mentality and the reality he encountered in Montreal. "They made us load pieces of scrap which were then sent to the foundry. The foreman called us all Joe. 'Hey Joe, come here, you!' And then he ordered: 'Take this stuff over there. Load this stuff on those trucks.' I remained there nine months; it was tough. I was not made for that kind of work; that was not work for artisans, but for day labourers." As soon as Funicelli managed to save a little money, he started a small shoe-repair shop, and later he even exploited his second trade, music, to organize his own group.[25]

Only a series of longitudinal studies of this urban immigrant work-force will reveal the different paths of the immigrant's economic integration, as well as the extent to which these became emancipatory itineraries. The pattern so far indicates more of an individualistic than a collective behaviour. Research in Montreal's daily newspapers over a thirty-year period shows that cases of collective action in the workplace involving Italian labourers are very rare, whereas conflicts involving a single worker are frequent. Some of these were marked by insubordination and sometimes even by violence. More often the worker just walked out, quitting his job and looking for a new one. Under such conditions the workplace did not function as a base for an emancipatory class strategy. This was related less to the existence of an incipient class consciousness in this type of immigrant worker and more to his working reality as well as to the use Canadian capitalism made of his labour.

Is it accurate then in this context to talk of "workers without a cause?" If the expression means that workers collectively sought to transform their wage-relation in order to increase their class power and to make the workplace a means of emancipation from capitalist exploitation, then clearly during this period Montreal's Italian labourers did not display a "workers' cause." If instead the work experience of these Italians is placed in the broader context of the "transcultural journey," of the immigrant experience as abandonment-reconstitution, of the immigration process as a life-cycle, then one can talk not of one "cause" but of a thousand: each with its subjective nuances, each with its sacrifices and humiliations, but also with its exploits and satisfactions. It is clear that this first generation of Italian immigrants did not transform Canadian capitalism into an emancipatory system; indeed they probably contributed to consolidate it and make it more functional. But it would be difficult to deny that in the process their lives changed; and when those changes took on a collective dimension, they left their permanent mark on the social and cultural life of a Canadian metropolis such as Montreal.

NOTES

1. See especially Robert Harney, "Men Without Women: Italian Migrants in Canada, 1880-1930," in B. Caroli, R. Harney, L. Tomasi, eds., *The Italian Immigrant Woman in North America* (Toronto, 1978); Robert Harney, "Montreal's King of Italian Labour: A Case Study of Padronism," *Labour/Le Travailleur* 4 (1979); Donald Avery, *"Dangerous Foreigners": European Immigrant Workers and Labour Radicalism in Canada, 1896-1932* (Toronto, 1979).

2. The emergence of a community infrastructure among Montreal's Italians is discussed in Bruno Ramirez, *Les premiers Italiens de Montréal: l'origine de la Petite Italie du Québec* (Montréal, 1984), chap. 1.

3. *La Presse*, 18 May, 1895.

4. *Royal Commission appointed to Inquire into the Immigration of Italian Labourers to Montreal and the alleged Fraudulent Practices of Employment Agencies* (Ottawa, 1905), 135-36.

5. *Ibid.*, 165.

6. Taped interview with Vincenzo Monaco, in Ramirez, *Les premiers Italiens*, 101-05.

7. *Ibid.*

8. *Royal Commission*, 165.

9. Taped interview with Costanzo D'Amico, April 30, 1979.

10. D. Viola, "Ispezione ai campi di lavoro di La Tuque," *Bollettino dell'emigrazione* 13 (1910), 27-28.

11. Taped interview, in Ramirez, *Les premiers Italiens*, 92-93.

12. Taped interview, *ibid.*, p. 115.

13. Sylvie Taschereau, "Pays et Patries: mariages et lieux d'origine des Italiens de Montréal, 1906-1930" (M.A. thesis, History, Université du Québec à Montréal, 1984).

14. Charles M. Bayley, "The Social Structure in the Italian and Ukrainian Immigrant Communities in Montreal, 1935-1937" (M.A. thesis, Sociology, McGill University, 1939).

15. *La Presse*, 9 December, 1897.

16. *Ibid.*, 30 December, 1904.

17. *Ibid.*, 18 and 25 May, 1895.

18. Our reconstruction of this incident and of its judicial and community ramifications is based on the coverage of *La Presse, La Patrie*, and the *Montreal Daily Star*, from 22 August, 1904 to 25 January, 1905.

19. Bruno Ramirez, "Montreal's Italians and the Socioeconomy of Settlement," in *Urban History Review* X, 1 (June 1981).

20. The phrase "emancipatory strategy" is understood to refer to working class consciousness and praxis which has as its objective the socialization of the means of production and end to capitalist exploitation. Eds.

21. Canadian Pacific, Montreal Office, Employee Pension Plan Files. (The author wishes to thank Mr. Omer Lavallée and Mr. Walter Gregory for their permission to consult these files).

22. Cf. Ramirez, *Les premiers Italiens.*

23. Taped interview, in Ramirez, *Les premiers Italiens*, 116.

24. *Ibid.*, p. 105.

25. Taped interview, in Ramirez, *Les premiers Italiens*, 125.

Beyond the Frozen Wastes: Italian Sojourners and Settlers in British Columbia*

Gabriele P. Scardellato

As recently as 1977 the state of Italian-Canadian studies was described as a "frozen waste," a terrain whose historiography, in particular, has been dominated by "pieties, filiopieties and errors in judgement."[1] Since that condemnation was issued, however, both its author, R.F. Harney, and others interested in the experiences of Italian migrants and immigrants in Canada, have done much to thaw the wasteland. Nonetheless, the progress of this thaw has been uneven. It has been felt most intensely in Quebec and Ontario or, more precisely, Montreal and Toronto. Outside of the country's heartland, the frozen wastes

* I would like to acknowledge the award of an Ethnic Studies Research Fellowship by the Secretary of State for Multiculturalism, which allowed me to carry out revisions to the preliminary version of this paper presented in Rome at the Canadian Academic Centre conference, May 1984.

remain virtually unaltered and usually only badly served by those filiopietistic studies which once sufficed for all of Canada. In the present study I will attempt to extend the thaw to Canada's western-most periphery, to the province of British Columbia.

My starting point is *The Italians in Canada* by A.V. Spada, one of the studies, which, while it epitomizes Harney's criticisms, also contains some useful information.[2] Spada devoted a chapter in his monograph to the history of Italians in British Columbia even though he claimed that "Italians have not made history..." in the province.[3] His chapter is organized as a geographical survey of a number of communities from Vancouver Island to the Alberta border where Italian immigrants settled. When possible Spada noted the arrival of Italian "pioneers" in these communities, the benevolent societies and similar organizations which they formed, and their entrepreneurial and other achievements. However, he devoted little attention to the migration process itself and his geographical approach confuses any chronological unity which the events described might have. My dissatisfaction with these aspects of his study led me to re-organize its contents in a way which would produce a more coherent chronological overview of the history of Italian migration and immigration to British Columbia. In turn, this re-organization suggested an hypothesis which might explain the pattern of settlement of Italians in the province.

The role of Canada's two major metropolitan centres, Toronto and Montreal, as migrant and immigrant destination or "targets" and labour distribution points, is well-known.[4] It seems unlikely, however, that Vancouver, the country's west coast metropolis, achieved a similar position in "the network of migration" in the period up to the

First World War. Instead, the evidence of British Columbia's settlement history suggests that the province presented Italian, and other migrants and immigrants, with two relatively distinct targets.

One of these was situated in the southwest corner of the province, on the Pacific coast. It was the first to develop, mainly through the impetus provided by the Fraser Valley and Cariboo gold rushes of the mid-nineteenth century. These attracted a significant influx of sojourners and settlers which not only contributed to the growth of the colonial capital of Victoria but also to that of its mainland counterpart, New Westminster, and to the growth of settlements like Nanaimo in the hinterland of these centres. This coastal region was based at first on an outward-looking, maritime economy whose horizons were the countries and settlements of the Pacific Rim.[5]

The other target was located in the southeastern and southcentral parts of the province and came to include a number of settlements situated along the international border from Michel at the Crow's Nest Pass to Trail, Rossland, and Grand Forks. This interior region was isolated from the coast because of the province's difficult terrain and its development began at a somewhat later date, in the late 1880s. The exploitation of the area's rich mineral resources, financed originally by American capital, was the primary reason for its growth. This capital was directed to the area through the metropolitan centre of Spokane in Washington state, the heart of the so-called "inland empire." As a result, the region's economy was oriented, for a considerable period of time, across the international boundary.[6]

As noted, the southwest coast region was the first to experience significant growth and this also drew the first

Italians to the area. They arrived with the gold-seekers of the Fraser Valley gold-rush of the 1850s along the same route followed by most other migrants or immigrants. This usually involved a transcontinental journey across the United States to San Francisco. The latter city, by 1851, had an estimated population of approximately 600 Italians.[7] Some of these sailed for Victoria and the Fraser River gold fields in 1858.

Their presence in the British gold camps is suggested by reports like that published in the *Victoria Colonist* in 1861 which described the good fortune of three Italian miners who left the colony after only three weeks with $12,000 in gold.[8] However, those whose careers can be traced in any detail from this very early migration settled in the colonial capital or in communities that grew up in its hinterland. Men like Carlo Bossi migrated with the gold seekers from San Francisco but ''decided that there was more to be made by supporting the gold fever than by succumbing to it.''[9] Bossi prospered as a merchant in Victoria.

Other early migrants like Giovanni Ordano or Francesco Savona moved further afield. Ordano settled near Cowichan on Vancouver Island, north of Victoria. His residence there from *circa* 1858 as a trader and hotelier is reflected in the name of Genoa Bay which commemorates his birthplace.[10] Savona, on the other hand, established himself on the mainland at about the same time. He operated a ferry on the route to the Cariboo gold fields at the west end of Kamloops Lake. Savona's Ferry, now known simply as Savona, recalls his adopted surname which in turn also commemorated his birthplace.[11]

In this colonial period of the region's history, long before construction of the Canadian Pacific Railway, access to the British territory which eventually became the province of British Columbia was very difficult. Nonetheless, Italians found their way to many of the region's settlements. Until the 1880s Victoria seems to have had the largest number of Italians in the new province but, as noted, others were located in its hinterland both on Vancouver Island and on the mainland as far away as the gold fields of the Cariboo. To the examples already cited we could also add those Italians who began to settle in the communities of the Vancouver Island coal fields in the 1870s or, in the same decade, in mainland communities like Kamloops.[12]

The construction of the CPR helped to reinforce this settlement pattern and also altered it in significant ways. The railway provided direct access to the province from central Canada and it offered both a means for travelling to it and, for those employed as navvies by the railway, a reason for doing so. Within the province new settlements were established along the railroad's right-of-way. Others, like the sawmill campsite originally known as Granville and incorporated in 1886 as the city of Vancouver, grew considerably because of its presence.

Italians were part of the CPR's multi-ethnic labour force in both its west-to-east and east-to-west construction crews. The evidence for their participation, like that for the gold-rush migration, is anecdotal rather than quantitative but nonetheless suggestive of a visible presence. Angelo Calori, for example, had reached Victoria via San Francisco in 1882. He worked for a time in the Vancouver Island coal fields before moving to CPR construction work on the mainland. Calori went on to establish himself as a hotelier in Vancouver shortly after the 1886 fire which destroyed much of the recently incorporated city.[13] The Italian merchants established in Victoria also sought to benefit from railroad construction work on the mainland.

Several of them, including Carlo Bossi, opened outlets in the settlements which boomed along the CPR right-of-way. In Yale, for example, described by an observer in 1881 as a bustling place whose streets were thronged with "[native] Indians, Englishmen, Swedes, Hindus, Italians, coolies and lots of Irish...,"[14] John Quagliotti Romano established the Romano House Saloon and Hotel. Romano had also been a clothing merchant in Victoria and a general provisioner in Nanaimo. On the mainland, besides his saloon-hotel, he also operated as a general provisioner in Lytton, north of Yale in the Fraser Canyon. In Lytton itself there were other Italians besides merchants like Romano. A certain Guido Magnone, for example, a self-described "artist," was resident there in the early 1880s. In 1883 he petitioned the Holy See in Rome for assistance in the construction of a Roman Catholic church in Lytton.[15] The proposed church might well have served men like John (or Giovanni) Sciutto, a general provisioner who also moved with the CPR construction crews. In 1885 Sciutto transferred his business from Yale to Kamloops where he entered into a partnership with two fellow countrymen; at least one of these had been resident in Kamloops for approximately ten years before Sciutto's arrival.[16]

Kamloops' prosperity and importance was enhanced by the arrival of the CPR and the railway's decision to establish a regional headquarters in the settlement. The town was already the site of one of the province's Oblate missions. The Residence of St. Louis had been founded in 1878 and some five years later Father Nicholas Coccola, O.M.I., one of its missionaries, was assigned to an unusual task.

The Oblates ministered to the needs of the CPR's

workers as the railway was built westward across the prairies. When construction reached the Rocky Mountains the Oblates in British Columbia continued with this mission. In particular, they noted the presence of "*beaucoup d'Italiens*" in the crews and responded by assigning missionaries for them who were fluent in Italian. Coccola, a native of Corsica, was one of these missionaries. From his Kamloops base he began his mission in 1883 and, as he later wrote, he spent several years ministering to the needs of "Italians and other catholic workers, spread out along... the railway line... over a distance of more than 300 miles."[17]

The completion of the railway provided British Columbia with a vital transportation link with the Dominion and, over time, this connection was instrumental in altering the economic orientation of the southwest coast from a maritime outlook to a continental one. The shift of the province's metropolitan centre from Victoria to Vancouver was a part of this process.[18] However, while Vancouver grew to supplant Victoria through the 1890s it does not appear to have attracted many Italian immigrants.

At the end of the nineteenth century Vancouver's population was approximately 27,000. This included a total of about 100 Italians who were engaged mainly as artisans.[19] This population, to be discussed in greater detail below, grew considerably in the period up to the First World War. However, this development was not unique in the province. Regional economic growth, particularly along the international boundary in the central and eastern interior, helped to produce equally significant Italian enclaves in areas which were geographically, and often politically and economically, remote from the metropolitan centre on the coast.

Some accounts of the history of Italian migration and immigration to the southern interior of British Columbia have singled out the activities of Father Giovanni Nobili, an Italian Jesuit missionary. He is credited with pioneering work in the Okanagan Valley in the 1840s which is said to have made "the Okanagan one of the principal centres of the small Italian settlement during the later years of the nineteenth century."[20]

It is the vineyards and orchards of this area of British Columbia which are often associated with the province's Italians.[21] However, the association is based on the exceptional and relatively late careers of a few vintners and their descendants; careers which only began to flourish in the 1920s.[22] More typical were the careers of those Italians who laboured on the railroads or in the mines and smelters further south and east of the Okanagan Valley, in the west and east Kootenays.

In the period 1887-95 the Kootenay region experienced a number of mining booms which began the exploitation of the area's rich mineral resources. These booms occurred without the benefit of direct Canadian rail links with either the Pacific coast or central Canada.[23] Instead, they were serviced with a flow of capital, goods, services and manpower which arrived via Spokane, the metropolitan centre of the "inland empire" built by men like the railway magnate, D.C. Corbin.[24] Its influence on southern British Columbia, in particular in terms of human traffic across the international border, was considerable.

This migration was a concern to the Oblates active in the area in the 1890s. From Nelson, for example, in 1893 one of them noted that the mining town of Kaslo, "*la Babylonne du West Kootenay*," with a population of

1,500 souls, would grow to five or six thousand with the emigration of miners, prospectors, speculators, gamblers and so forth from Spokane, Portland and Seattle.[25] In the same year he noted with some exasperation not only the physical isolation of the region from the rest of British Columbia, but also the outlook that this produced in its inhabitants. "When I talk about sending... children," he wrote, "either to Kamloops or New Westminster people smile and ask: Where are Kamloops and New Westminster? When I explain they decide to send their children to Spokane!"[26]

Of course, the isolation and resultant lack of knowledge about the geography of the province may have been irritating only for organizations like the Oblates. These, after all, were dependent on bases which lay in the hinterland of the Pacific coast. Those who laboured in the hinterland of the "inland empire" appear to have been content to be within reach of a centre like Spokane. Through the latter they had access to the United States via the extensive American railway system which provided migrants and immigrants, like its counterpart in Canada, with employment opportunities. The Veltri brothers migrated to the Kootenays after this type of employment in the United States.[27]

They reached the inland empire in the late 1880s where they were employed on the construction of D.C. Corbin's Spokane Falls and Northern Railway to the Canadian border.[28] When that was completed they crossed the border into British Columbia where they took up contracts for railway work around Kaslo, then further south at Rossland and so forth. The Veltris worked in the region for almost a decade and then shifted their base of operation to Winnipeg. For many others, however, the railways, mines and smelters of the Kootenays proved to be sufficent for their needs.

Giovanni Veltri noted in his memoirs that the mines around Rossland were worked "*per lo più*" by Italians. No figures are available but a strong Italian presence in communities like Rossland is suggested by the creation in 1899 of the province's first mutual aid society, the Giordano Bruno.[29] An equally important Italian enclave was begun in these years a short distance east of Rossland in the settlement of Trail. The town was built at the foot of the bluff on which Augustus Heinze built his famous smelter, at the confluence of Trail Creek and the Columbia River.

"Isacco and Caterina Giorgetti arrived in 1895 when the town was little more than a huddle of shacks along the river and the... smelter had not yet been blown in."[30] These appear to have been the first of a substantial number of Italian immigrants who began to settle in Trail from the end of the nineteenth century.[31] Like the Giorgettis many of them reached Trail via Spokane and the latter remained an important distribution point for migration to the Kootenays even after the CPR had completed its southern branch through the Crow's Nest Pass.[32] The completion of a Canadian route to the region was extremely important in ending its isolation, at least from eastern Canada, and the new railway contributed to the growth of a number of Italian enclaves in settlements along its right-of-way. For Trail, the CPR's purchase of Heinze's smelter was equally important, given the railway company's employment of Italians in its section gangs. Many Italian navvies found more permanent work in the company's smelter and their settlement in Trail contributed to the growth of the town's Little Italy.[33] Even before the turn of the century the town had an Italian-owned and operated hotel. By 1900 Italian grocery stores had been established and in 1905 the *Società Mutuo Soccorso Cristoforo Colombo* was founded.[34]

The latter was the third to have been established in the region. It was preceded by the Giordano Bruno of Rossland and the *Società Emanuele Filiberto, Duca d'Aosta*, founded at Michel near the Crow's Nest Pass in 1903. This, the second oldest of British Columbia's Italian mutual aid societies, drew its membership from those Italians employed in the coal fields of the east Kootenays. They formed a significant component of the workforce of companies like the Crow's Nest Pass Coal Company, so much so that by 1910 they were able to form another mutual aid society in the coal fields, the *Fior d'Italia*, established in Fernie, on the CPR line to the west of Michel.[35]

By the beginning of the twentieth century, therefore, there were two relatively distinct regions in the province which could be seen as targets for Italian migrants and immigrants. The coast region was perhaps the most dynamic of the two as its new metropolitan centre, Vancouver, grew in step with the re-orientation of the area's economy from a maritime to a continental outlook. This development was important for the movement of Italian migrants and immigrants to the metropolis and its hinterland. Where, for example, west to east construction of the CPR in the 1880s had attracted Italian navvies via San Francisco and/or the Vancouver Island coal fields, by the beginning of this century the CPR in the province could contract for its labour in the metropolitan centres of central Canada.

The self-styled "King of Italian Labour," the *padrone* Antonio Cordasco, for example, was well aware of the CPR's manpower needs in British Columbia, even though he was based in Montreal, and he played an active role in satisfying them. In the early 1900s he intervened in the competition between two Boston firms which sought to provide Italian labourers for the CPR in British Columbia. He warned one of the firms "that there was no point in recruiting people" for this labour market "because he, Cordasco, was sole agent for that railway and he would only order manpower through" the other rival firm.[36] Cordasco's claim was not an empty one. At his self-celebratory banquet in 1904, when he crowned himself "King of Italian Labour," "most of the foremen in attendance were impressed by the presence of the chief superintendent of the CPR's Vancouver division. After all, that gentleman would be hiring 5000 or 6000 Italians during the coming spring, and he seemed to be... honouring his friend Cordasco."[37]

The interest shown by men like Cordasco in the labour needs of the province and their ability to integrate the region in the international network of migration and its "*commercio di carne umana*"[38] is further evidence of the "new consciousness of British Columbia in the minds of eastern business interests"[39] which developed from the end of the nineteenth century. Other agents in the "network" also began to devote some attention to conditions in British Columbia at about this time. When they did so, they reported, possibly unknowingly, the division of the province into the two regions or targets outlined above.

There was little differentiation in Italy, at least before World War II, between Canada and the United States as destinations for Italian emigrés.[40] Nonetheless, the Italian government had commissioners of emigration who were based in the United States and these sometimes reported on Canadian conditions as did other agents. The

Italian Consul in Montreal in 1901, for example, was able to provide his government with information about a fictitious colonization company called the "Cootenay [*sic* Kootenay] Association" based in Fernie, British Columbia, which seems to have been little more than a labour agency.[41] In 1902, the same year in which this report was published, the Commissioner based in New York, *cavaliere* Egisto Rossi, was sent to study conditions in Canada for Italian migrants.[42] His investigations were confined to Quebec and Ontario, but in a brief reference to the absence of Italian workers in the mines of central Canada he noted that in British Columbia, "*la maggior parte degli Italiani sono impiegati nelle miniere*," and that they were settled in particular concentrations in "Vancouver, Nelson, Fernie, Victoria, *ecc.*"[43] A few years after Rossi's report the *Commissariato dell'Emigrazione* published another which dealt much more specifically with Italians in British Columbia.

In 1910 Amy A. Bernardy completed the second of two trips which she undertook for the *Commissariato* to study the welfare of Italian women and children in the United States. She toured the central and western states and by late February 1910, on the second to last leg of her trip, she had reached Seattle, Washington. There she found that her return journey to St. Paul, Minnesota, on the Northern Pacific Railway was blocked because of snowslides. Faced with an eight to ten day wait she decided to follow "the last open route" eastward, the Canadian Pacific from Vancouver. Because of this decision, she wrote, "I was caught up in the disaster of the Glacier [British Columbia] snowslide [of 4-5 March 1910]...." With the other survivors she was forced to backtrack westward to Revelstoke. There, by means of "the most mediocre trains and steamers'' she was able to continue her journey by travelling down the Arrow Lakes and then eastward to Cranbrook and southeastward into the United States and so back to St. Paul.[44]

Bernardy's detour into British Columbia prompted her to include the Italians of the province in her report. She noted that there were several ''colonies'' or enclaves on Vancouver Island: a very small one of 30 to 40 Italians in Victoria; another of 400 to 500 in Nanaimo; and a ''strong nucleus'' of Piedmontese miners in Ladysmith.[45] For mainland settlements she singled out Vancouver as having a ''*Piccola Italia*'' with a population of 1,500 manual labourers which included many Calabrians and a few Venetians while Fernie (which she incorrectly identified as one of the *colonie* of Vancouver Island) had ''... *un vero* 'settlement' (*colonia*) *calabrese di 600 a 1000 persone*.'' This overview of Italian settlement in the province appears to be based on information gathered during her stop in Vancouver. And, in this instance at least, it seems doubtful that she was able to verify her findings *in situ*.[46] Her informants in Vancouver[47] seem to have been unable to provide her with much information about Italian settlements outside the southwest region of the province: further evidence, perhaps, of the isolation of the two regions outlined above.

According to Bernardy, by 1910 Vancouver's Little Italy had been established in the city's east side, in the vicinity of Westminster (now Main) Street: an area which she described as the most rundown of the city. The neighbourhood, she reported, was made up entirely of small houses of five to seven rooms and the crowding was such as to force as many as ten or twelve people to sleep per bedroom. Consequently, the houses were very dirty but sanitary conditions nonetheless were "*assai buone*!" There were few families living in more "decorous" conditions even though many labourers had property worth from one to two thousand dollars.[48] She added that three-quarters of the colony was without family and therefore was housed by the remaining quarter. Boarders paid from four to six dollars monthly for a bed, laundry and heating, and they usually bought and prepared food independently of the boarding household to avoid exploitation.[49]

Vancouver's Italian enclave grew considerably in the first decade of this century. The city's first Italian mutual aid society, the *Società Mutuo Soccorso Figli d'Italia*, was established in 1905, five years before Bernardy's visit.[50] In the same year the Oblates purchased and reconsecrated as the Church of the Sacred Heart a former Protestant church in the neighbourhood. Two years later they assigned to the new parish a pastor, François Lardon, O.M.I., who was fluent in Italian as well as French and English.[51] A number of Italian grocery stores, an Italian bakery and similar enterprises were also begun in this period.[52] And in 1911, a second association, the *Società Veneta*, was formed and the first Italian language newspaper, *L'Italia nel Canada*, was published in the city.[53] In the same year the Roman Catholic Archbishop of Vancouver, the Most Reverend Neil McNeil, prompted by the number of Italians in his archdiocese, attempted to create an Italian parish for them. He began his effort with a letter to the then Apostolic Delegate in Ottawa, *Monsignor* P. F. Stagni.

Archibishop McNeil wrote to *Monsignor* Stagni in December 1911 for assistance in finding an Italian priest who could be entrusted with the care of "over four thousand Italians" that he claimed were then resident in Vancouver. He had been approached by the 200 odd immigrants from Castelgrande, Potenza, who had supplied him with the name of a young priest from their "native place who would be glad to come to Vancouver." The Archbishop sought information about the priest and guidance from the Apostolic Delegate on the creation of an Italian parish. McNeil also alluded to the "numerous" Italians throughout the remainder of his diocese and expressed his particular concern that many of those in Vancouver had lost their faith and "that very many spend their Sundays drinking beer and whiskey, and hence quarrels and scandals."[54] The Apostolic Delegate responded promptly.

He advised Archbishop McNeil "to make arrangements with some religious community to care for... [Vancouver's] Italians." Stagni was himself a Servite and he suggested that his order, with experience of two Italian missions in Chicago and one in Denver, "would be inclined to accept some missionary work for the Italians in Canada."[55] This suggestion brought the Provincial of the Servites in Chicago, Father H.B. Heil, into the correspondence. The latter, in letters to both his Superior General in Rome and the Apostolic Delegate in Ottawa, revealed a good general knowledge of western Canada, "said to be developing faster than any other region of America," and of the importance of Vancouver, "destined to become one of the most important ports on the Pacific Coast."[56]

Monsignor Stagni, for his part, was even better informed about conditions in British Columbia and Vancouver in particular. In a letter from Ottawa to his Superior General, for example, he accurately described both the role of the Oblates in the history of the province and the growth of Vancouver. From the 1880s, he wrote, when the city "did not yet exist," it had grown to its present level with a population of over 130,000. He attributed this growth to Vancouver's position as the terminus of the "great Canadian railway, the CPR, a line which crosses the entire continent from Montreal to Vancouver."[57]

The effort to create a parish for Vancouver's Italians and the manner in which it was undertaken is further evidence of an increased awareness of the province and its metropolitan centre.[58] This is also reflected in the beginnings of a Servite mission in the city which was marked with the consecration of the Church of Our Lady of Sorrows in 1912.[59] The new church was an offshoot of the Servite monastery of the same name in Chicago. And, in some respects, its introduction to Vancouver resembles the influx of branch companies from central Canada, or the heart of the continent, to the Pacific seaboard.[60]

In the first decade of this century, and up to the First World War, both target regions in the province grew considerably. As they did, so too did their Italian enclaves. However, it is important to note that the regions remained isolated from each other and that as late as 1916, "B.C.'s coastal cities still had little commercial presence" in the southcentral and southeastern interior.[61] This isolation was caused, to a large extent, by the lack of a straightforward transportation link. Amy Bernardy's re-routing to the south and east after the Glacier avalanche exemplifies the difficulties that existed for travellers who attempted to travel between the regions. Until 1916, when the long-awaited Kettle Valley Railway was completed, the situation was equally difficult for travellers from outside the province. However, some observers appear to have been unaware of this problem.

The *Commissariato dell'Emigrazione*, for example, published a report on British Columbia in 1915. Produced by the Italian government's attaché for emigration based in Montreal, it lacked detailed familiarity with conditions in the province.[62] The attaché provided information on British Columbia's resources, the wages that might be earned in various sectors of the economy and so forth, but his only specific remark about Italians concerned "the very large number" who were employed in mining and related activities in the province.[63] He concluded with advice for would-be émigrés who might want to travel to the province. The route he recommended involved railway journeys from the ports of Boston or New York and he quoted railway fares from the latter as $37.10 to Fernie, $40.70 to Revelstoke, $43.85 to Kamloops, $49.85 to Vancouver and $50.85 to Victoria.[64]

This list of railway ticket prices for destinations in British Columbia ignored local realities and, in particular, the isolation from each other of the province's two most developed regions.[65] That isolation, however, and the location of each region to the capital and labour distribution centres of central Canada and the United States, were essential in determining the movement of Italian and other migrants and immigrants in the province. From eastern Canada, for example, from about the turn of the century, migrant labourers could have been expedited to either region but until 1916 there was no straightforward means by which they could be directed between regions within the province. Thus, through one of the most important periods of Italian mass migration to North America, British Columbia's emerging metropolitan centre could not serve as the labour distribution point for the entire province.[66] The evidence for sojourning life in Vancouver in the first fifteen years of this century suggests that the city's Little Italy was produced by the same forces that formed its counterparts in other metropolitan centres in the country, but its role in this respect was confined to its own, relatively limited hinterland. Sojourning labourers in the southcentral and southeastern interior were unlikely to have wintered in the city.

An awareness of the pattern of regional growth and settlement in British Columbia is essential for an understanding of the parallel growth of the province's most important Italian enclaves. It is also useful for an understanding of how some enclaves could be established towards the end of an important period of mass migration and how some of these could continue to flourish when conditions for immigration to Canada were less than ideal. A good example of this phenomenon is provided by the community of Powell River, a coastal settlement some 130 kilometres north of Vancouver.[67]

The Powell River Company which built the town was formed in 1909 and in the same year it began construction of its pulp, paper and lumber mill, and of a dam across Powell River for hydroelectric power. The Company produced its first newsprint from its new mill in 1912 and by that date it had also completed about fifty permanent houses in the townsite that it was building for its employees.

Company employment and similar records as well as those of the community's Roman Catholic parish, reveal an Italian immigrant presence in the Company's workforce from the first years of its history.[68] The first of these were migrant construction workers, perhaps sojourners who returned to Vancouver when their labour was no longer needed. Very few of them stayed on for employment in the pulp and paper mill which they helped to build. The Company's employment of Italian-origin labourers peaked in 1929 when approximately 150 Italians were on its payroll. Through the Depression this component of the Company's labour force was cut by more than one half, but in the decade which preceded that upheaval a flourishing Italian enclave was established in Powell River. This is reflected in the formation of an Italian benevolent society in 1924 with a membership of 300, followed a few years later by an Italian grocery store as well as an Italian barbershop and poolhall.[69] The Italians who formed this enclave can be traced in their journeys to Powell River through the Company's employment records.

In these the Company noted, where possible, an employee's previous employer and place of employment. Those Italians who were hired before 1920 were almost evenly balanced between recent arrivals in Canada whose last employment, for example, was noted frequently as "just out from Italy" and those who had worked in or near Vancouver before moving to Powell River. The significant exception to this pattern occurred in 1917 when, for the first time, the Company hired three Italians who previously had been employed in the southcentral and southeastern interior.[70] In the 1920s, that is in the decade in which Canadian immigration policy was tightened concurrently with its counterpart in the United States, there was a decline in the number of employees hired who were said to be "just out from Italy."[71] However, this decline was almost counterbalanced by the increase in the number of those hired from the previously isolated settlements of the southern interior.

The number of newly arrived Italians hired by the Company in the 1920s fell to below one-quarter of the total number of all Italians hired in the decade. Those who had worked in Vancouver or its hinterland, including settlements on Vancouver Island, formed approximately 40 per cent of the total while those who had worked in Alberta or other provinces represented fourteen per cent of the total of Italians hired. Italians from communities in southcentral and southeastern British Columbia represented some 20 per cent of all Italians hired by the Company in the decade.

Thus Vancouver and the settlements of its hinterland were important sources for the Powell River Company's supply of Italian labourers. Migrants and immigrants travelled through the metropolitan centre en route to Powell River or they laboured in the city or its hinterland before migrating to the company town. This labour distribution network in the province was extended considerably after the two main target regions were connected with a direct railway link. After this the Company could draw labourers from settlements as distant as Michel, Fernie or Trail. Future research will have to incorporate the role of local conditions in both target regions as part of an analysis of Italian migration between them. For the moment I can only emphasize again the importance of the parallel growth of Italo-Canadian enclaves in both regions in the province. Their existence helps to explain how an entirely new enclave could be formed in Canada, on its westernmost periphery, even after the severe disruption of Italian emigration to Canada in the 1920s.

NOTES

1. R.F. Harney, "Frozen Wastes: The State of Italian Canadian Studies," S. Tomasi, ed., *Perspectives in Italian Immigration and Ethnicity*. (New York, 1977), 115-31, 122.

2. A.V. Spada, *The Italians in Canada/Les Italiens au Canada* (Ottawa, 1969).

3. *Ibid.*, 358-85. His chapter incorporates, often *verbatim*, an unpublished study, *The Italians in British Columbia* written by Rachel Giese and dated December 1966. She produced this with "... material gathered by the *Comitato Attività Italiane*, Vancouver, with grateful thanks to... Mr. Ermès Culòs of Powell River and Mr. Nello Picone of Trail." *Ibid.*, 368 noted the existence of the *Comitato* and recorded Giese as one of a lengthy list of "Italian professional and businessmen residing in Vancouver," *ibid.*, 370-71, without reference to the *Comitato's* research or Giese's paper.

4. *Cf.* R.F. Harney, "The Padrone System and Sojourners in the Canadian North, 1885-1920," G.E. Pozzetta ed., *Pane e Lavoro: The Italian American Working Class* (Toronto 1980), 119-37; "The Commerce of Migration," *Canadian Ethnic Studies*, IX, 1 (1977), 42-53; "Boarding and Belonging," *Urban History Review* VIII, 2 (1978), 8-37; Bruno Ramirez, "Montreal's Italians and the Socioeconomy of Settlement, 1900-1930: Some Historical Hypotheses," *Urban History Review* X, 1 (1980), 39-48; with Michael Del Balso, *The Italians of Montréal: From Sojourning to Settlement, 1900-1921* (Montréal, 1980).

5. Robert A.J. McDonald, "Victoria, Vancouver and the Economic Development of British Columbia," W. Peter Ward & Robert A.J. McDonald, eds., *British Columbia: Historical Readings* (Vancouver, 1981), 370-95.

6. *Ibid.*, 375-76.

7. This figure was reported in *l'Eco d'Italia* of New York, 26 April 1851, as cited in Andrew Rolle, *The Immigrant Upraised: Italian Adventurers and Colonists in an Expanding America* (Norman, Oklahoma, 1968), 256. Rolle also noted that "several hundred" of these were Ligurians who had arrived in San Francisco on ships carrying coal from England, *loc. cit.*

8. *Victoria Colonist* of 14 October 1861 cited in Fred Ludditt, *Barkerville Days* (Langley, B.C., rev. ed. May 1980), 31. The Italians, not named in the report, were returning from the Cariboo gold fields.

9. John Norris, ed., *Strangers Entertained; A History of the Ethnic Groups of British Columbia* (Vancouver, 1971), 141.

10. G.P.V. Akrigg & Helen B. Akrigg, *1001 British Columbia Place Names* (Vancouver 1973, 3rd. ed.), 70, where his arrival at Genoa Bay is dated in 1858. Spada, *Italians in Canada*, 362, dates Ordano's arrival in 1856.

11. Akrigg & Akrigg, 153, "Francis or Francois [or Francesco?] Savona... was an Italian whose name was so difficult for non-Italians to pronounce that he... adopted the name of his birthplace as a substitute surname."

12. Spada, *Italians in Canada*, 376.

13. Giese, *Italians in B.C.*, 2, Spada, *Italians in Canada*, 367.

14. Cited in Pierre Berton, *The Last Spike: The Great Railway, 1881-1885* (Toronto 1971), 211.

15. Archives of the Sacred Congregation of *Propaganda Fide, Scritture riferite in Congressi*, 1883-84, folios 837-47. I am very grateful to Dr. Roberto Perin, Atkinson College, York University and former director of the Canadian Academic Centre in Italy, Rome, for bringing this material and that cited below, note 54 *et seq.*, to my attention.

16. Spada, *Italians in Canada*, 375.

17. *Ibid.*, 376-78, based on K. Cronin, *Cross in the Wilderness* (Toronto 1960), 191-212. Spada states (377) that Coccola was ordained at St. Mary's Mission, Colorado, misinterpreting Cronin (193), who describes his ordination "by Bishop D'Herbomez [of British Columbia] in 1881 at St. Mary's Mission [Mission City, B.C.]. Coccola died in 1943 (Cronin, 212), not in 1934 (Spada, 379). Coccola's letter describing his work with CPR navvies was published in *Missions De La Congrégation des Oblats de Marie Immaculée* 24, 95, (*septembre* 1986), 297-313, and is dated "*Saint-Louis Kamloops 10 février* 1886."

18. McDonald, "Victoria," 370.

19. Norbert MacDonald, "The Canadian Pacific Railway and Vancouver's Development to 1900," Ward & McDonald, ed., *British Columbia*, 396-425. The figures cited are taken from the 1901 Census and reproduced by MacDonald on 414-15.

20. Norris, *Strangers*, 141, where Nobili's efforts in the 1840s are connected with the arrival of John Cosorso [*sic* Casorso or Casorzo] in the valley of Mission Creek at Okanagan Mission in 1883. However, the latter mission had been founded and developed by the Oblates, beginning with the efforts of Father Charles Pandosy in 1859, (Cronin, *Cross*, 66 *et seq.*). Casorso first travelled to the Okanagan in Pandosy's company and worked for the missionaries at Mission Creek before beginning his own ranching and other enterprises. *Cf.* Victor Casorso, *The Casorso Story: A Century of Social History in the Okanagan Valley* (Okanagan Falls, B.C., 1983).

21. Harney, "Frozen Wastes," 118.

22. Norris, *Strangers*, 142.

23. McDonald, "Victoria," 375-76.

24. John Fahey, *Inland Empire: D.C. Corbin and Spokane* (Seattle, 1965).

25. Julien-Augustin Bédard, O.M.I., letter dated at Nelson, B.C., "*janvier* 1893," Oblate Archives, Rome.

26. *Ibid.*

27. Giovanni Veltri's career is briefly recounted in F.C. Hardwick, ed., *From an Antique Land: Italians in Canada* (Vancouver 1976), 31-32.

28. Giovanni Veltri, "*Ricordanze Autobiografiche* — Autobiography of a Self-Made-Man" (typescript, Grimaldi, Cosenza 1955), 4-13. I am indebted to Prof. R.H. Harney of the Multicultural History Society of Ontario (MHSO) for placing this manuscript at my disposal. *Cf.* Fahey, *Inland*, 80 *et seq.*, for the construction of Corbin's railway north out of Spokane, starting in the spring of 1889. David L. Nicandri, *Italians*

in Washington State: Emigration 1853-1924 (Washington State American Revolution Bicentennial Commission 1978), 36 *et seq.*, for an overview of the history of Italians in Spokane and their employment on railroad construction.

29. Veltri, "Ricordanze," 8, Giese, *Italians in B.C.*, 7, and Spada, *Italians in Canada*, 379. Additional, if unflattering, evidence for the presence of Italians in the region is provided by Edmund Kirby, manager of the War Eagle Consolidated Mine of Rossland who wrote, in a letter of 31 January 1901, "How to head off a strike of muckers or labourers for higher wages, without the aid of Italian labour, I do not know." Laurier Papers, Public Archives of Canada, cited in Martin Robin, *The Rush for Spoils: The Company Province, 1871-1933* (Toronto 1974), 45.

30. Giese, *Italians in B.C.*, 10. Spada, *Italians in Canada*, 380, incorrectly dated the Giorgettis' arrival in 1855, while in Norris, *Strangers*, 142, they are noted as "Issaco and Caterina Giogetti."

31. Giese, *Italians in B.C.*, 12-3, lists a number of early immigrants but does not provide biographical or similar information for them. The list is repeated with some additions and spelling errors in Spada, *Italians in Canada*, 380.

32. Giese, *Italians in B.C.*, 12-3, for the careers of Paolo Muzzin and "Joe" Le Rose.

33. Giese, *Italians in B.C.*, 11-2, for the career of "Pete" Lauriente, also reproduced in Norris, *Strangers*, 143 and Spada, *Italians in Canada*, 384.

34. Giese, *Italians in B.C.*, 14, Spada, *Italians in Canada*, 384. The significance of ethnic grocery stores and similar enterprises in the creation of an Italian *ambiente* and Little Italy is amply discussed by a number of authors, *cf.*, R.F. Harney, "*Ambiente* and Social Class in North American Little Italies," *Canadian Review of Studies in Nationalism* 2:2 (Fall 1975), 208-24, John Zucchi, *The Italians of St. John Ward, 1875-1915: Patterns of Settlement and Neighbourhood Formation* (Toronto 1981), and Ramirez & Del Balso, *Italians of Montréal, passim.*

35. Giese, *Italians in B.C.*, 7, Spada, *Italians in Canada*, 385.

36. R.F. Harney, "Montreal's King of Italian Labour: A Case Study of Padronism," *Labour/Le Travailleur* 4 (1979), 57-84, 78.

37. *Ibid.*, 76. In the same study, 68, Harney describes Cordasco's efforts to expedite skilled stonecutters from Udine to work as labourers in British Columbia, a fate which they refused.

38. Harney, "The Padrone System and Sojourners," 121.

39. McDonald, "Victoria," 384 *et seq.*

40. R.F. Harney, *Italians in Canada* (Toronto, 1978), 8.

41. "L'Immigrazione nel Canada durante l'anno 1901," *Bollettino dell'Emigrazione*, no. 9 (Rome, 1902), 36-40, 38. Hereafter cited as *Bolletino*.

42. "Delle Condizioni del Canada rispetto all'immigrazione italiana, Rapporto inviato dal cav. Egisto Rossi, Commissario dell'emigrazione in missione," *Bolletino*, no. 4 (Rome, 1903), and dated "*Nuova York, novembre* 1902."

43. Rossi, *Delle Condizioni*, 10.

44. Amy A. Bernardy, "Sulle condizioni delle donne e dei fanciulli italiani negli Stati del Centro e dell'Ovest della Confederazione del Nord-America." *Bolletino*, no. 1 (Rome 1911), 3-170. Her detour in British Columbia is recounted on 6. The frontispiece map published with her report suggests that she travelled from Seattle to Vancouver via Victoria although the latter is incorrectly placed on the Olympic peninsula in Washington State.

45. *Ibid.*, 25-26.

46. *Ibid.*, 10.

47. These are not named in Bernardy's report but she does refer, in an anecdote about the exploitation of an Italian woman in Vancouver who ran a boarding-house, to the "*regio agente consolare*," as well as "*un prete Italiano*" in the city, *Ibid.*, 78.

48. *Ibid.*, 70.

49. *Ibid.*, 78. Boarding and other aspects of life in Vancouver's Little Italy are recounted in interviews in D. Marlatt & C. Itter, "Opening Doors: Vancouver's East End," *Sound Heritage* VIII, 1-2 (Victoria 1979). Violet Teti Benedetti, 33-6, for example, born in Vancouver in 1906, recalled that her mother ran a boarding-house with two kitchens, one for her family and the other for her boarders. She did the latter's laundry but not their cooking. See also R.F. Harney, "Boarding and Belonging," *Urban History Review* VIII, 2 (1978), *passim*, for a detailed analysis of the boarding phenomena. Boarding costs in Toronto *circa* 1911, at three dollars per month, appear to have been cheaper than those in Vancouver, *Ibid.*, 24.

50. Giese, *Italians in B.C.*, 2-3, Spada, *Italians in Canada*, 367, Marlatt & Itter, "Opening Doors," 29. One of the founders, Angelo Calori, has been discussed briefly above, 139.

51. A.-G. Morice, O.M.I., *Histoire de l'Église Catholique dans l'Ouest Canadien*, 4 Vols. (Montréal 1923), vol. 4, 375-79. "*... le nouveau curé* [*Lardon*] *possédait... la langue italienne. Il en profita pour soigner d'une manière toute spéciale les Italiens, assez nombreux dans sa paroisse, et pour lesquels rien de particulier n'avait jamais été tenté*," 377. For Father Lardon's career in British Columbia see his dossier in the Oblate Archives, Rome.

52. For the importance of these types of enterprises in the formation of Little Italies see above, note 34. Their growth in Vancouver's enclave is documented in various interviews in Marlatt & Itter, "Opening Doors," *passim*.

53. Giese, *Italians in B.C.*, 6, Spada, *Italians in Canada*, 369, and Norris, *Strangers*, 143, for the appearance of *L'Italia nel Canada*, a weekly published by Angelo Fuini. Given its name, the *Società Veneta*, founded by Filippo Branca, an immigrant from Turbigo, west of Milan, seems unlikely to have been formed as "a close-knit association of men from [Branca's]... native province," Giese, *Italians in B.C.*, 3 and Spada, *Italians in Canada*, 367. Norris, *Strangers*, 143, possibly from Spada or Giese, describes this *Società* as a "specialized organization for migrants from Venetia [*sic Venezia or the Veneto*?]." The biographer of Filippo's son, Angelo Branca, describes the association as having been formed "for northern Italians," see Vincent Moore, *Angelo Branca, "Gladiator of the Courts"* (Vancouver 1981), 15.

54. McNeil to Stagni, 15 December 1911, *Archivio Generale dell'Ordine dei Servi di Maria* (AOSM), Rome.

55. Stagni to McNeil, 21 December 1911, AOSM, Rome.

56. Heil to Stagni, 9 January 1912, ASOM, Rome.

57. Stagni to his Superior General, 16 *Gennaro* 1912, AOSM, Rome. The Apostolic Delegate visited the province in 1913 as described in a letter, again to his Superior General, of 13 *Luglio* 1913, AOSM, Rome.

58. Significantly, the Archbishop who began the initiative was himself a "migrant" from the east. Prior to his elevation to the archbishopric of Vancouver in February 1910, Archbishop McNeil had been bishop of St. George, Nfld., Morice, *Histoire*, 379-80. As Stagni noted, *loc. cit.*, he was the first non-Oblate bishop to be appointed to a diocese in the province.

59. Morice, *Histoire*, 390, describes the consecration of "*Notre-Dame des Sept-Douleurs*" on 2 November 1912. He speculated that it was assigned to the Servites who had been in the country for only a short time because "the apostolic legate to Canada, Mgr. Stagni, was a Servite." Giese, *Italians in B.C.*, 5 and Spada, *Italians in Canada*, 369, date the consecration of Our Lady of Sorrows in 1913.

60. This is not to deny the religious, humanitarian and similar motivations which prompted the effort to create an Italian parish. For the influx of companies see McDonald, "Victoria," 384-87.

61. *Ibid.*

62. Girolamo Moroni (*R. Addetto dell'emigrazione in Montreal*), "Il British Columbia (Canada)," *Bollettino*, no. 1 (Rome, 1915), 67-79.

63. *Ibid.*, 74-6. Much of his report reads as if it could have been compiled from a decent almanac or similar publication.

64. *Ibid.*, 79. He quoted these as "Immigrants' Fares" to which an immigrant was entitled for up to fifteen days after his arrival in the United States. After this fifteen-day period an immigrant was liable to the full second class fare. Moroni may have quoted these American fares because, as he noted, the government of Canada provided neither free nor reduced-price tickets for immigrants.

65. The attaché did note, *ibid.*, 69-70, that the district of Vancouver was the most populated and developed in the province followed by the Kootenay district which was "very developed both in agriculture and industry (minerals and lumber)."

66. Harney, *Italians in Canada*, 8 for migration trends to North America.

67. This community and its Italian enclave is the subject of a study by the author titled "Italian Immigrant Workers in Powell River, B.C.: A Case Study of Settlement before World War II," *Labour/Le Travail* 16 (Fall 1985), 145-63.

68. These records are discussed in detail in *Ibid., passim*.

69. *Ibid.*, 148, 161, Giese, *Italians in B.C.*, 9 and Spada, *Italians in Canada*, 374.

70. Two of these were former employees of the smelter in Trail and the third had been a quarryman in Grand Forks.

71. Harney, *Italians in Canada*, 25, for the "contagion of xenophobia and racialism" which prompted the restrictionist attitude in Canadian immigration policy in the 1920s. Franc Sturino, "Italian Immigration to Canada and the farm labour system through the 1920's" *Studi Emigrazione* XXII, 77 (March 1985), 81-96, for a wider discussion of restrictionism and the immigrant response to it. Scardellato, "Italian Immigrant Workers," 157-58, for the use of the "farm labour system" by employees of the Powell River Company as an immigration and migration strategy.

Italian Art and Artists in Nineteenth-Century Quebec: A Few Preliminary Observations*

Laurier Lacroix

Italian immigrants made a name for themselves in a variety of endeavours during the last century, but their contribution to artistic creation remains little known. By a strange ideological turnaround, there is a kind of taboo that keeps us from understanding the culture of the time. How can we — and indeed, why should we? — inquire into the influence of nineteenth-century Italy, a country creating art in decline, on Quebec's art, colonized and full of European and American influences? Traditional art history cares little about the exchange between two insignificant partners, which is why little has been said about the issue. Algebra renders a positive result when we add two negatives, but art history does not display the same tolerance and arithmetical precision.[1]

* Translated by David Homel.

To look into the subject at all implies rejecting some prejudices. First, we have to accept a definition of art which is concerned with more than the avant-garde and that parade of masterpieces we have been conditioned to appreciate. We must consider art as esthetic production that can satisfy different levels of tastes and fulfill a variety of social roles: education, moral instruction, decoration, propaganda. The esthetic object which in itself evokes formal interest is part of an economic network involving apprenticeship of a trade and its techniques, commissions and contracts, and marketing and distribution. Such an inquiry accepts the existence of "peripheral" activities outside artistic centres and Masters' studios — those traditional arbitrators of Art.

These premises are a prerequisite to the examination of artistic relations between Italy and Quebec in the nineteenth century. There are other factors too that have conspired against the subject, one being the fragmented state of nineteenth-century studies. As well, Canadian art historians, with their modernist and ethnocentric ideologies, have paid greatest attention to the relations of artists in Canada with their two mother-countries and the United States. The kind of art we will consider portrays historical painting, religious subjects treated in paint and sculpture, ephemeral funerary art and decorative art, using such base materials as plaster and cement — subjects snubbed by traditional art history. We are far from the splendours of the Renaissance and Baroque which, having been made into museum pieces, were torn from their original context and meaning.

Before progressing further, we should make a few comments about method and facts. We use the word "Italy" for the sake of convenience only; in Italian art, regional differences influenced the type of production. As well the notion of a national art,[2] in Quebec as in Canada, is not tenable. Dividing the nineteenth century up into set periods also creates problems. While we can date the arrival of the first immigrant artists in Quebec, and thus define the temporal parameters of our topic, the phenomenon which we are studying is part of a more complex social and ideological current, more difficult to compartmentalize, but which must be kept in mind. Artistic relations between Italy and Canada did not develop linearly since the two countries were not privileged partners (Canada sought its artistic sources in France, England, Belgium, Holland, Germany and the United States); each country took advantage of particular circumstances in the other.

The sources in our bibliography are not very eloquent: these include a few travel diaries and documents published at the time, such as parish monographs. Most later publications denigrate this type of art history, dismissing it out of hand as academic, insipid, lacking in inspiration, repetitive and tedious. This essay seeks to reopen the file and consider the works themselves, the circumstances of the artists' arrival in Canada, and the way their works were commissioned.

It is important to situate the presence of Italian artists in Quebec in the wider perspective of the knowledge and perception that Canadians had of Italian art. This perspective, while not directly tied to any one artist, will help us better to understand the expectations of the Canadian public in relation to immigrant artists, and to assess the impact of the Italian presence in Canada. We must look at two sources: information published in periodicals and other contemporary texts, often based on the experience of Canadians travelling in Italy; and the works themselves, together with the networks that were used to import them from Italy. Though we will not dwell on them, these sources constitute the background for the cases which will be examined.

Pierre Savard has given us an overall view of the awareness and image of Italy in nineteenth-century French-Canadian culture. The research and writings of art historian Gérard Morisset allowed Savard to conclude that "le arti visive devono molto all'Italia" (visual arts owe much to Italy). From articles and travel accounts, Savard discovered that there were two Italies:

> ... la prima è l'Italia "eterna," quella che la natura ha privilegiato e il cui patrimonio artistico e culturale è estremamente ricco. ... La seconda Italia, è l'Italia moderna, che li [Canadian travellers to Italy] interessa poco, o di cui aborriscono la politica anticlericale.[3]

Research into the periodical literature[4] of the time confirms Savard's conclusions. Attention centered primarily on Classical and Renaissance Italy; contemporary production was scarcely mentioned at all. This literature celebrated the way of life and art of that Golden Age that ran from Renaissance Florence to seventeenth-century Rome. The values of Roman antiquity, with its well-oiled colonial machine, appeared as models to this nostalgic age which only praised with equal fervour the grandeur of Christendom and its masterpieces. Articles dealt mostly with the discoveries at Pompeii, the expansion of the Roman Empire, the art of the Quattrocento and the Vatican collections. Artistic societies founded in Canada after 1860 regularly organized illustrated lectures on the art of the fifteenth and sixteenth centuries. Romanesque art would not be "discovered" until the end of the nineteenth century, and only a few major contemporary events (the construction of the Vittoriano, the Italian participation in various world exhibitions) were mentioned in Canadian periodicals.

The appearance of the mass circulation illustrated press after 1870 increased the awareness of Italian art, even as it changed the consumers' pictorial habits. Sixteenth- and seventeenth-century original or copied engravings used as interior decoration and as a source of inspiration for artists in Canada continued to be widely imported during the first half of the nineteenth century.[5] This kind of work was finding its way into collections at a time when the mass circulation of reproductions in the daily press, and in publications sponsored by religious communities, made available what was once known only through literary descriptions. This is how works by artists such as Titian, Correggio, Reni, Michelangelo, Domenichino, Veronese, Parmigianino and, of course, by far the most popular, Raphael were distributed. This network while supposedly celebrating the eternal values of the Beautiful, used reproductions in periodicals as "ready-mades" to serve as illustration and propaganda. *L'Opinion Publique*, for example, circulated in December 1871 ten thousand copies of a *Virgin and Child* by Carlo Dolci (Galleria Corsini) with the title "Don't wake him up." Apart from the special significance of publishing the image at that particular time of year, we can imagine how such works predisposed the judgement and taste of Canadians to share the esthetics of Italian artists who claimed to be the heirs of the rich cultural tradition that they were being asked to reactivate in Canada.

Italian works coming to Canada took three major

routes. The first was through merchant-auctioneers, wholesalers and specialists who occasionally imported works, and whose flyers advertised a hodge-podge of imported goods including Bologna sausage, lava from Vesuvius, mosaics, marble tables, engravings, paintings and sculptures. These merchants contributed to the consumers' appreciation of Italian culture. Gérard Morisset has already tried to situate the careers of merchants like Martinucio (whose activities can be followed between 1823 and 1835) and Balzaretti[6] (active from 1819 to 1848). A native of Merlina in the Como region, Balzaretti was well integrated into the French-speaking intelligentsia. He was president of the *Société française au Canada* from 1842-43 and, as such, chairman of the celebrations for the feast of St. Napoleon.

The clergy were another channel for importation, especially of contemporary works into Canada. The *collèges classiques* were notable in this respect, as were church councils which were always keen on regularly upgrading the quality of their decorations. Every priest and bishop who travelled to Italy for educational or business purposes never failed to return with a work, either as a souvenir or as a decoration for a church.[7] The taste for such art spread. Even if they did not make the trip personally, priests could place their orders through a representative of their community or a member of the Canadian clergy working in Rome in an administrative capacity. A goodly number of stations of the cross came to Canada this way.[8] Abbé Benjamin Pâquet, future rector of Laval University, frequently stayed in Rome (1863-66; 1873-78; 1886; 1888-89). He helped popularize the work of Vincenzo Pasqualoni (1819-1880),[9] fifteen of whose works can be seen in Canada. Meanwhile, the Jesuits and the archbishop of Montreal encouraged the famous Pietro Gagliardi (1809-1890) by commissioning portraits of the popes, the Montreal episcopate and a variety of religious subjects. In Quebec, the presence of works by artists such as Carlo Porta, Ippolito Zapponi and Giorgio Szoldaticz (figure 1) prove there was a network that deserves to be reconstructed.[10]

Apart from dilettantes and patrons, there were more serious collectors, both secular (figure 2) and religious[11] who exposed the Quebec public to Italian works. The Desjardins collection was brought to Canada in 1817 and again in 1820. Of its 180 imported paintings, more than twenty works were attributed to the Italian school. The most revealing example, even if it occurred in Ontario, points to the didactic value conferred upon "classical" art. Egerton Ryerson, superintendent of education in Canada West, formed an educational museum at the Toronto Normal School in the 1850s and 1860s.[12] The museum was comprised almost totally of copies of works taken from Florentine museums, some of which were executed by a compatriot, Antoine-Sébastien Falardeau (1822-1889), a professional copyist who had lived in Florence since 1846.

This sensibility and attraction to classical Italy was reinforced by numerous visits to Italy by Canadian artists in the nineteenth century. We have now been able to catalogue ninety-eight Canadian painters who, prior to 1914, sojourned in Italy (the number would be greater if we added the architects and sculptors who have not yet been enumerated). The chronology and purpose of these visits provide a way of organizing and interpreting this impressive figure. Relatively few artists went before 1880, but the ones who did, stayed for a longer period of time (three to five years). The increased ease of transportation and the large number of Canadians going to Europe to complete their training after 1880 account for the greater presence of

Canadian travellers in Italy. Some of them registered at Italian schools. Others went to study in a more unstructured environment and took advantage of their long stay to seek out treasures in museums and public buildings and to copy them. The majority, however, were short-term visitors, lured by nature and the charm of certain centres.[13] They took advantage of the climate to paint *al fresco*, or sketch works they found attractive. The repercussions of their visits could be felt in a number of ways. They influenced the teaching of art (Edmond Dyonnet, for example), the awareness of Italian art (copies, lectures, texts) and the overall familiarity with Italian culture and sensibility. As a result, artistic judgement became more refined, and Italian artists in Canada could be either appreciated, competed against or rejected more intelligently.

Artists from a variety of Italian provinces were active in Quebec from the 1820s onward, though there were too few of them to see in their presence the signs of an artistic movement. The date a given work was begun or an important piece commissioned tells us about their rhythm of production. After 1860 family or friends already established in Canada helped these artists,[14] who came mostly from the northwest provinces of Italy, in the settlement process. They specialized in monumental works: murals, frescoes and statuary. The pre-1870 wave of artists did not necessarily leave Italy to come to the British colony. Their careers were like those of itinerant artists who, despite quality training, had to travel from city to city in search of commissions due to the constraints of their local markets (figure 3). Because of the costs involved in murals and sculptures, and the length of commissions, these artists became quasi-sedentary; some made Montreal or Quebec City their home port.

We have so far been able to identify more than thirty artists of Italian origin active in Quebec before 1914 (table 1). Almost one-third were working in murals and decoration; the others were in statuary, funerary sculpture and decorative arts. Mural painters and decorators introduced a new concept of public decor into Canada. Unfortunately, these artists' creations have been destroyed in part or in whole, making their examination and evaluation much more difficult. The execution of a mural creates special problems that no artists active in Canada up to that time had been able to resolve. The development of a unified iconographic and decorative cycle, the harmony between a building's function and the theme of the decoration, as well as the formal integration of the decoration to the building which houses it were challenges the muralist had to face. In this medium, the Sulpicians were pioneers. They called upon Angelo Pienovi (Genoa, 1773 — Montreal, 1845) to decorate the brand new neo-Gothic Notre Dame church in Montreal in 1828. The earliest decoration of Notre Dame (no longer visible today) probably repeated the stencilled geometrical motifs on the columns and vault, in the way that people of the time imagined Gothic cathedrals originally had been decorated. On September 19, 1833 Pienovi put an advertisement in *La Minerve* that serves as our introduction to him:

> Angelo Pienovi, of Genoa, Italy, who painted the new parish Church, and the Church of the Grey Nuns of Montreal, informs the public that he is ready to accept works in his domain, that may be offered to him, such as: Churches, architectures, Salons, Landscapes, decorations, in oil or temper.

The ability to adapt both to private and public decor (including theatre sets), to express different types of subjects, and in different media, can be observed in the advertisements placed by later artists[15] who continued the tradition inaugurated by Pienovi. The career of Luigi Cappelo, which developed somewhat later, is a good example and demonstrates that the expectations of Italian artists remained the same. Born in Turin in 1843, Cappelo travelled throughout Italy after studying at the Academy of Fine Arts in his native city. In 1874, he was teaching drawing at the Collège Sainte-Marie de Montréal, which may indicate he came to Quebec at the instigation of the Jesuits. He had a successful career as a decorator (figure 4), portraitist and easel painter, and left behind works in a dozen churches throughout Quebec.[16] Cappelo adapted well to his new country: he married a French-Canadian woman, Marie-Louise Lebrun, and took the young Ozias Leduc as an apprentice, teaching him the rudiments of a type of art that his compatriots had been practising in Quebec for nearly sixty years. In fact, after 1860, Italians were forced to share the flourishing mural-painting market with German-born and native Quebec artists. Competition became tougher as the latter learned the techniques and were teaching them to others.[17] Not that the contribution of the Italians ended there. The prolific Florentine artist Guido Nincheri (1885-1973), active in Quebec as a muralist and glass-maker from the middle of the 1910s onward, succeeded in creating an extremely rich and varied formal and iconographic universe, of great originality, the pride of various churches and private buildings today.[18]

Though we do not yet have a catalogue of works, we know a considerable amount about Italian artists in Quebec and their activities as sculptors, statuette makers, and statuary artists. Their production is a testimony to the ingeniousness and hard work employed by sculptors to win new commissions. The rapid increase of new associations, often with short life-spans, together with the fact that techniques were transmitted in studios some of which spanned several generations[19] were expressions of a hierarchical social organization and a structured division of labour, most of which was craft-oriented and technical. In Montreal, the Catelli firm (whose activities began in 1853) was associated from 1864 to 1867 with the sculptor G. Baccerini. In 1867, Catelli formed a new association with Tommasso Carli, who came to Canada in 1858 (figure 5), and who had been employed by Baccerini. Baccerini was to pass his business on to Filippi in 1880. Alessandro Carli, son of Tommasso, joined the Petrucci Brothers in 1923, a statuary company that had its beginnings in Montreal in 1910. A break-off group was born from this association, Petrucci and Carli, which remained active until 1972. Based at Wolfe and Montcalm streets, dozens of employees worked in studios, carrying on the tradition of "middle-brow" art, supported by the clergy.

Italian artists took advantage of an expanding market in which a new material — plaster — was winning converts among buyers and institutions. Less expensive and easier to work than wood, which was the traditional material in Quebec, plaster-cast objects were made popular as much by Italian statue-makers as by pieces imported from France and Germany. Making the molds took some creativity, though earlier parts were often re-used in a new product. But pouring the plaster and applying the paint did not demand great skill. In any case, a variety of factors insured the popularity of Italian statue-makers and won them the lion's share of the market. Among these factors were new marketing techniques (the use of illustrated publications, so that products could be advertised and sold through the mail) together with the great flexibility of plaster. Works of different sizes could be provided, using subjects which expressed the whole range of devotions of parish or community life. Plaster began to dominate middle-brow art (figure 6) and those sculptors who used wood or paper maché were forced to imitate the finish and colour of plaster works.[20] Italians also gave Quebec poured-concrete statues, recommended as being especially suited to the harsh climate. And Italians were also prized for a more noble activity: stone-cutting. They used these talents in construction and funerary sculpture.

Even though this subject is under-developed in the field of art history, it tells us much about nineteenth-century visual culture. Italian artists may have given us only a handful of exceptional works, but they profoundly influenced popular taste and its manifestation in both public and private practices of devotion, and more importantly in the conception of mural art. United by origin and a knowledge of common techniques, these artists contributed to culture in Quebec by providing the clergy with products they were able to integrate and use for nearly a century. This kind of symbiosis between the patrons of art, the artists and the consumers is suspect to conventional art history; it conjures up a facile, academic, conservative kind of art, designed for lovers of kitsch. As if only the intellectual avant-garde deserved to be studied! The awareness and definition of a culture may well be obtained through its most innovative aspects, but we must also pay heed to mass movements and commonly shared attitudes. In this context, the participation of Italian artists in the life of our society is an asset we can no longer ignore.

NOTES

1. Until very recently, art history texts had nothing to say about nineteenth-century Italian art between the neo-classical sculptor Canova and the Futurists; it was all a vast void. Gérard Morisset, who did not appreciate the second half of the nineteenth-century, attacked Italian artists in Quebec in these terms: "Bad taste imported from Italy has taken over our churches and won't let go..." *Peintres et tableaux* (Quebec City, 1936), 1, 124.

2. Corrado Maltese in *Storia dell'arte in Italia 1785-1943* (Turin, 1960) points out the opposition in Italian art after 1855 between "regional schools" distinguished by Romanticism and Realism, and a movement that spanned the entire territory that would be influenced by *al fresco* painting and the Impressionists. Each tendency claimed that it alone defined national art. See the article by Giovanni Previtali on the section "La periodizzazione della storia dell'arte italiana" that describes the development of the perception of a "national" art in the historiography of Italian art history. *Storia dell'arte in Italia 1785-1943*, I (Turin, 1979), 5-95. Enrico Castelnuovo and Carlo Ginzburg, in a chapter entitled "Centro e periferia" (pp. 285-352), explore the problem of the multiplicity of centres of production in Italy and their interaction through time.

3. Pierre Savard, "L'Italia nella cultura franco-canadese dell' Ottocento," *Canadiana: Problemi di storia canadese* (Venice, 1983), 93.

4. My cataloguing is not systematic, and far from complete. It is largely based on the material published under the direction of Hardy George, *Index to Nineteenth Century Art Periodicals* (Concordia University, 1981), and on the cataloguing done by the National Gallery of Canada, which includes, for example, *Canadian Illustrated News* (1869 and 1883) and *L'Opinion publique* (1870-1883).

5. John R. Porter of the History Department of Université Laval is documenting this phenomenon by examining the periodicals of the time. The collections of teaching institutions such as the Séminaire de Québec and the Ursuline convent in Quebec City have additional material.

6. Gérard Morisset, *La peinture traditionnelle au Canada français* (Ottawa, 1960), 83.

7. As impossible as it sounds, entire church decorations were commissioned from artists who never set foot in Canada. Antonio Petriglia executed 22 paintings for the decoration of the Saint-Louis de France church in Montreal (1895-96). A few rare cases are documented of religious patrons who not only imported works into Canada, but artists too. In 1847, Monsignor Bourget brought back the young painter Ettore Vacca (born in 1828), who died shortly after his arrival in Montreal.

Local artists disapproved of the practice of importing religious works and artists; Antoine Plamondon (1804-1895) wrote several articles for the local press undermining the credibility of these artists and their work. He published the following letter in *Le Courrier du Canada* on July 1, 1870: "The letter of XCVIII by the celebrated Louis Veuillot, dated Rome, May 19, and entitled 'L'exposition romaine' published in your issue number 58, must have surprised those two or three gentlemen from Quebec City who, over the last several years, have been expending unusual efforts to keep our venerable country priests from having their church paintings done by Canadians rather than having them made in Rome by Italians. Louis Veuillot is an illumination to us all, a man of unimpeachable integrity, clear-headed judgement and refined taste; what does he think of these Roman artists, painters and statue-makers? You have read it; the venerable priests have read it too. Let them reread it now..." Plamondon takes Veuillot to witness as to the mediocrity of contemporary Italian religious art.

8. Giovanni Silvagni for Notre Dame in Montreal (ca. 1845); Ruspi (1867) for the church at Lévis; Antonio Petriglia (ca. 1897) for St. Patrick's church in Montreal. See Yves Lacasse on Silvagni's stations of the cross, *Antoine Plamondon: Le chemin de la croix de l'église Notre-Dame de Montréal* (Montreal Museum of Fine Arts, 1983), 42-5, figure 10.

9. Archives of the parish of Saint-Georges de Beauce, Benjamin Pâquet à Fernand Catellier, 6 décembre 1875. "Rome, French Seminary/Dear Friend, As soon as I arrived in Rome, I went to visit the painter Pasqualoni to see how the paintings are going with my own eyes. St. Catherine is finished. The painting is very beautiful. The death of St. Joseph is well along; it too will be a fine painting. The sketch for the painting of St. George is done: I'm very pleased with it. The Immaculate Conception is finished." Abbé Pâquet comments on the latter work, and says there is no angel in it, contrary to what his friend had hoped for. If he wants one, he will have to pay extra. (Guy-André Roy told me of the existence of this letter, and I thank him for his help.)

10. The low value of Italian currency is not without relation to this movement. Based on statistics I have gathered, it appears to have cost less to commission a work from a reputed Italian artist working for members of the clergy than from a Quebec artist. The art market was more highly developed in Italy, and competition resulted in lower prices.

11. *Archivio Propaganda Fide, Scritture Riferite in Congressi America Settentrionale*, vol. 15, John James Lynch to Cardinal Préfet Franchi, 25 May 1877, relating a literary evening at the Université Laval in honour of the Holy Father, marking the visit of Monsignor Conroy to Quebec City, describes the uses of a work of art: "A superb portrait of Pius IX on a heroic scale set at the rear of an immense hall, surrounded by garlands and crowns, dominated the audience which was like one great family gathered around a beloved Father."

12. See Fern Bayer, *The Ontario Collections* (Toronto, 1984), 7-37.

13. In the years after 1890, Venice inspired a great amount of interest. William Brymner described the city in these terms: "The general colour of Venice is a grey rose colour running into all kinds of other greys, and old faded greens and yellows. These colours lighted by the late afternoon sun reflected into the gently undulating canals, with the black gondolas to give a positive note to the delicate general tone, makes a wonderful harmony. Add to this the graceful shape of the buildings, thus coloured and you have the most unique combination of beauty I have ever seen." See the catalogue prepared by Janet Braide, *William Brymner, 1855-1925: A Retrospective* (Kingston, 1979), 49-50, and David McTavish, *Canadian Artists in Venice 1830-1930* (Kingston, 1984).

14. See, for example, the study of the Carli family done by John R. Porter and Léopold Désy, "Les Statuaires Carli et Petrucci," *L'Annonciation dans la sculpture au Québec* (Quebec City, 1979), 125-37.

15. On the many talents of Gerome Fassio (Rome, 1810 — Bytown, 1851), see David Karel's article in the *Dictionary of Canadian Biography* VIII (Toronto, 1985), 320-22. F. Pedretti displayed his talents by executing "fresco paintings" in the concert hall of the Bonsecours Market (*La Minerve*, 7 March 1854). Almini decorated the Windsor Hotel in 1877.

16. Among the most interesting works that remain, see those in Notre Dame church in Montreal; Saint-Isidore in Laprairie; Pointe-Claire; Saint-Paul l'Ermite, Saint-Rémi de Napierville and the Ursuline chapel in Trois-Rivières.

17. Napoléon Bourassa (1827-1916) trained several artists of this type during the decoration of the chapel of Notre-Dame de Lourdes in Montreal (1880). The rudiments of mural painting were also taught at the schools of the Conseil des Arts et Manufactures and at the Monument national. See Laurier Lacroix, "La peinture murale dans les églises au Québec," *Sessions d'études, Société canadienne d'histoire de l'église du Canada* 47 (1980), 95-98.

18. Among the works by Guido Nincheri, see the decoration of the Château Dufresne and the churches of Saint-Viateur in Outremont, Saint-Léon in Westmount, Chiesa della Difesa (Montreal) and the stained glass windows of the Trois-Rivières cathedral.

19. Porter and Désy, "Statuaires."

20. See, for example, the *Sacré-Cœur* (1877) executed by Louis Jobin (1845-1928), reproduced in the reprinting of Gérard Morisset's *Le Cap-Santé, ses églises, son trésor* (Montreal, 1980), 321. Also see Mario Béland, *Louis Jobin, maître sculpteur* (Musée du Québec, 1986), 121. Béland qualifies this kind of sculpture this way: "The statuary is characterized by its insipid attitude and expression of the characters, the floppy draping and the loud colours of the painted surfaces."

1. Giorgio Szoldaticz (1873-?), *Portrait de Mgr. Paul Toussaint Larocque*, oil on canvas, painted in Rome around 1895, Archevêché de Sherbrooke. (Photo: Musée du Québec)

2. Giovanni Maria Benzoni (1809-1873), *Buste de Georges-Étienne Cartier*, marble, done in Rome in 1867, Assemblée nationale du Québec. (Photo: Louise Leblanc, Service des ressources pédagogiques, Université Laval)

3. Gerome Fassio (1810-1851), *Portrait de Jean-Baptiste Godin*, miniature, 1848, Musée du Saguenay-Lac Saint-Jean. (Photo: Mychel Monfette)

4. Luigi Cappelo (1843-after 1899), *Rideau de scène de la salle de spectacle du Collège de l'Assomption*, 1883, taken from Anastase Forget, *Histoire du Collège de l'Assomption*.

5. Edmond Dyonnet (1859-1954), *Portrait de Thomas Carli*, oil on canvas, 1892, Montreal Museum of Fine Arts. (Photo: MMFA)

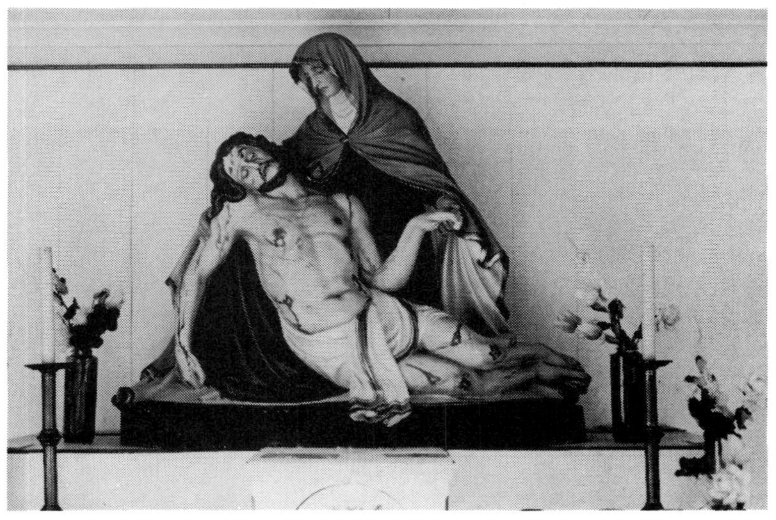

6. M. Rigali (there is documentation of the Rigali firm in Quebec City between 1880 and 1890), *Vierge de pitié*, painted plaster, 1885, Saint-Laurent, Île d'Orléans. (Photo: Inventaire des Biens culturels, 81.1241.15(35))

Table 1
Artists of Italian Background Active in Quebec prior to 1918

	Artist	Dates	Activity
1	Almini, M.	active late 1870s	painter
2	Baccerini, G.	active 1862-1880	sculptor
3	Caccignaci, E.	active ca. 1880	sculptor
4	Cantara	active ca. 1880	architect
5	Carli, A.	1875-1952	statuary
6	Carli, A.	1881-1968	statuary
7	Carli, C.	1894-	statuary
8	Carli, G.	1848-1928	statuary
9	Carli, T.	1838-1906	statuary
10	Carli, U.	1889-1929	statuary
11	Carli, V.	1873-1929	statuary
12	Carnevali	active ca. 1890	painter
13	Carta, L.	active ca. 1880	architect
14	Catelli, C.	1817-1906	sculptor
15	Cernichiaro	active 1890-1910	goldsmith
16	Cerusi	active ca. 1901	statuary
17	De Feo	active ca. 1857-58	painter
18	Deprato	active ca. 1914	glass-maker
19	Donati, P.	active ca. 1820	mold-maker
20	Donato, G.	active ca. 1908	sculptor
21	Fassio, G.	1810-1851	painter
22	Filippi, P.	active ca. 1880	sculptor
23	Giovanelli, P.	active ca. 1916	sculptor
24	Marchi, A.	active ca. 1916	sculptor
25	Mariotti, C.	active ca. 1875	sculptor
26	Pedreti	active ca. 1855-60	painter
27	Petrini	active ca. 1880	painter
28	Petrucci, A.	1887-1950	statuary
29	Petrucci, N.	1890-1960	statuary
30	Pienovi, A.	1773-1845	painter
31	Rigali, M.	active ca. 1880-90	statuary
32	Schinotti, G.F.	active ca. 1830	decorator
33	Sciortini, F.	active ca. 1918	sculptor
34	Sula	active ca. 1865	sculptor
35	Vacca, E.	1828-1847	painter

The Italians of Quebec: Key Participants in Contemporary Linguistic and Political Debates*

Paul-André Linteau

In 1968, in the small Montreal suburb of Saint-Leonard, the language question sparked violent incidents between Italians and French Canadians. The issue was the following: should the municipality's Italian immigrants be forced to send their children to French schools or should they be left free to choose their language of instruction? The conflict stirred passionate debate, turbulent meetings and street battles between members of the two groups.

The episode marks an important stage in the Quebec political and language debates of the sixties and seventies. The issues extend beyond the situation in Saint-Leonard, reflecting the larger context of changes in Quebec society during this period: the rise on the one hand of a new Quebec nationalism and the affirmation on the other of the

* Translated by Sherry Simon.

"allophone" groups — those that are neither French nor British in origin. Italians are the largest of these groups. They were drawn into the centuries-old struggle between French and English Canadians in Quebec. They became the focus of a conflict which at first was not of their own making, but in which they came to play an active role by defending their own positions with respect to the new Quebec nationalism.

In this paper I focus on certain aspects of the context which defined relations between Italians and French Canadians after the Second World War and especially after 1960. Over the last few years, sociologists, political scientists, linguists, economists and demographers have formulated many hypotheses about the socio-economic and socio-linguistic life of immigrant groups in Quebec, with particular attention to the Italians. It is now possible to explain — from the inside, as it were — the development of the Italian community in Quebec over this period.[1]

But this development must also be explained in terms of the larger context of the transformations of Quebec society and its traditional way of handling ethnic and linguistic relationships. It is impossible to deal adequately with this question without plunging into the historical roots of these relationships. My perspective will be fundamentally historical. It is important to keep in mind that American models of immigrant adaptation cannot be applied as such to the Quebec situation.

Towards Ethnic Diversity

To understand the situation of Quebecers of Italian origin during the period which concerns us, we must first look back at the main patterns of settlement in Quebec and the various migratory and ethnic trends affecting the formation of this population.

It is not necessary to go back as far as the seventeenth century and the foundation of New France to define the two main trends which characterized the growth of Quebec's population in the nineteenth century. The first was the proverbial birthrate of the French Canadians which resulted in a significant population increase throughout the century, even creating a demographic surplus. Unable to find work in Quebec, the surplus population emigrated in large numbers to the United States and specifically to New England. The second trend was the strong flow of immigrants from the British Isles to Quebec between 1815 and 1860. The immigrants were mainly Irish but also English and Scottish. By the middle of the nineteenth century they made up a quarter of Quebec's population.[2]

The rapid decline in this immigration after 1860, coupled with the high birthrate of French Canadians, raised the French-Canadian proportion of the population to 80%. This level was maintained throughout the first half of the twentieth century.

As a result of these demographic trends, the ethnic composition of Quebec was rather simple, unlike elsewhere in North America. At the end of the nineteenth century, the Quebec population was composed essentially of Catholic French Canadians and a British group formed of two major constituents: Irish Catholics and English and Scottish Protestants. Other ethnic groups numbered only a few thousand individuals and accounted for less than 2% of the total population.[3]

The situation began to change significantly at the turn of the twentieth century. Two major waves of immigration, one preceding the First World War, the other during the twenties, increased the numbers of the British group. More and more of these immigrants were English and Scots, whereas the Irish underwent a marked decline. In the long run, however, the most dramatic change was the diversification of the population settling in Quebec through the arrival of immigrants from countries other than France or Britain. East European Jews were the largest group with Italians, Germans and other Europeans in much lesser numbers. By 1913 they collectively made up 6% of the population.[4]

These figures might seem negligible, but they take on new significance when we note that these newcomers almost all settled in Montreal. Also, during the second half of the nineteenth century, the British, who were once found in almost all regions of Quebec, gradually withdrew to Montreal. For example, whereas they once accounted for 40% of Quebec City's population, today they number only 4%. Montreal became much more cosmopolitan than the rest of Quebec. French Canadians barely exceeded 60% of the population; the British constituted another 25%, and in 1931 the other groups formed 13.7% of the population of the Island of Montreal.[5]

These waves of immigration ended with the Depression and the Second World War. Once again the demographic weight of French Canadians increased. But the end of the War brought a new period of intense immigration. While Quebec still attracted a certain number of British immigrants and large contigents of displaced persons from Eastern Europe, post-war immigration to Quebec included more and more people from Mediterranean countries. The most numerous of these were the Italians. By 1960 they had become the largest non-British and non-French ethnic group.

During the sixties and seventies, the ethnic diversity of Quebec grew even stronger with the arrival of immigrants from North Africa, the Caribbean and Southeast Asia. By 1971 ethnic groups which were neither British nor French made up 10.4% of the total population. (This was almost the same percentage as the population of British origin.) These ethnic groups made up 20% of the population of Greater Montreal and more like 25% of the Island of Montreal. The increase in population among these groups after the War inevitably had a profound effect on Quebec society, especially because the immigrants were concentrated in Montreal. During the sixties they began to be called *allophones* to distinguish them from the francophones and the anglophones.

It is important to see the increase in these new populations in relation to the relative decline of the dominant groups. The decrease in the British population began in the nineteenth century and was accentuated by the move westward of Canadian economic activity. The drastic fall in the French-Canadian birthrate began in 1965 and changed the long-standing balance between the two groups. The major increase in the numbers of new groups came at a time when the two traditional groups were at an important turning point. We can understand then that the allophones came to play an important role in the uneasy relationship between French-Canadians and English-Canadians in Quebec.

Despite the diverse origins of the allophones who arrived after the War, the group is still composed — as it was since the beginning of the century — of two major categories. More than half are either Jewish or Italian in origin. The majority of immigrants during the first half of the twentieth century were Jews; after the War they were

Italians. The Italian population increased from 34,165 in 1951 to 108,552 in 1961, making it the largest ethnic group neither French nor British in origin. By 1971, Italians accounted for about 3% of the Quebec population, almost 6% of the Greater Montreal area and 7.6% of the Island of Montreal. They are now estimated to number more than 160,000 in Greater Montreal. Given these figures, it is not surprising that Italians should have been at the heart of the ethnic and linguistic debate in Quebec over the past decades.[6]

Strategies for Managing Ethnic Relations

Ethnic relations for many decades in Quebec were basically a dialogue between English and French. Only late in the twentieth century did these relations become diversified. The long history of ethnic relations in Quebec therefore tells a very distinctive story — that of a land where, for over a century, two groups of European descent shared majority status, even if their numbers were far from equal. What made this relatively harmonious and durable coexistence possible was a clearly defined strategy of ethnic relations which took the form of a great historical compromise, begun in 1840 and completed at Confederation in 1867.

The pact was agreed to by the leaders of both communities and it aimed at putting an end to several decades of tension and conflict. On the one hand the French-Canadian elites gave up their strong nationalist demands and claims to political autonomy. They agreed not to hinder and in some cases to support the economic goals of the mainly Anglo-Scottish bourgeoisie. For its part, the bourgeoisie gave up its dreams of assimilating the French Canadians and left French-Canadian leaders enough political and cultural power to allow for the survival of the ethnic group.

Confederation in 1867 confirmed this pact by granting the francophone majority in Quebec some degree of political autonomy, especially in the areas of education, culture and local issues. In return Anglo-Protestants obtained a number of political and constitutional guarantees intended to protect their cultural institutions from any changes which might affect the majority.

This great historical compromise sought to minimize ethnic frictions which had reached their peak with the clash of arms in 1837-38. The very deliberate means chosen to reach this goal was a strategy of institutional separation based on both ethnic group and religion. Each large ethnic and religious group would be supported and contained by its own institutions: churches, schools, colleges, universities, hospitals, welfare institutions, charities, and so on.

Quebec became characterized by a multitude of separate and parallel institutions. The most extreme fragmentation occurred in charitable and other private institutions; the public education system, however, retained a relatively simple structure. The system was officially divided into two sectors but in practice there were three: the Anglo-Protestant and the Catholic which in turn, was subdivided into a main branch for French Canadians and a secondary branch in English for the Irish. These ethnic separations were complicated by an additional, unofficial, separation based on social class. Within each network, institutions intended for the mass of the population were distinct from those which served the elite.

This strategy is a far cry from the American melting pot. The ethnic partitioning of Quebec was in fact a kind of anti-melting pot. Without declared aims of assimilation, the system sought to minimize friction between groups by reducing the points of contact between them. It aimed to ensure that each group could, if it so wished, remain safe from outside influences and develop according to its own norms. The effects of this well-entrenched system inevitably had a profound effect on the management of ethnic relations at a time when in the late twentieth century these became more diversified.

Could a system based on separation and discrimination survive the arrival of new groups? During the first half of the twentieth century it adapted quite well. The newcomers were mainly Jews and Italians. Out of their long experience of persecution, the Jews rebuilt in Montreal a series of institutions brought from Europe. The Italians, although not as well structured, could count on the Church to provide them with specific services including priests of their nationality. Synagogues and Italian Catholic parishes dispensed specific social and cultural services, adding to Montreal's institutional diversity.

For the public education system, however, this ethnic diversification posed a particular problem. Should new school systems be created, even though the constitution offered guarantees only for Catholics and Protestants? The problem was most pressing for the Jews who were of a different religion. But after lengthy debate they were integrated into the Protestant school system which turned into a *de facto* non-Catholic system. The Jewish people of Quebec gradually learned English, but this of course did not mean that they were integrated or assimilated into the British minority. They formed a very distinct cultural group in the city, subject to discrimination in the school system which took various subtle forms. It was only after the Second

World War that the barriers of discrimination were definitely eliminated.[7]

The old strategy of ethnic separation continued to function until the War. It was bolstered by a further social distinction between new and established immigrants. Montreal was a city of ethnic isolation, a multitude of separate cultural universes.

While the system succeeded in keeping communities separate, one might wonder if it did the same on the individual level. In their daily lives Montrealers would of course have dealings with neighbours, merchants, superiors and work companions of different ethnic origins. How were these cultural contacts experienced over time and what were their long-term effects? We know very little at the moment about such fundamental questions; cultural and ethnic historians should be encouraged to explore them.[8]

We have seen then that the newly settled communities in Montreal at the start of the century reinforced the institutional strategy developed by French and English-Canadian leaders. The detailed story of the Italians provides us with a particularly interesting illustration of this point.

The Development of Italian Community Institutions

The context in which the Montreal Italian community developed encouraged strong internal cohesion. The work of Bruno Ramirez and Sylvie Taschereau demonstrates the importance of family and neighbourhood relations. The Italians who came to Montreal in the first third of the twentieth century were mainly from Molise and Campania, often from neighbouring *paesi* in these regions. The institutional network they set up soon after their arrival fostered the integration of newcomers into the community. Boarding houses and corner food stores played an important role in this respect.[9]

The Catholic Church was also important in promoting social cohesion among the Italians of Montreal. Even before the First World War, the Italians had two national parishes, each with its priests and associations. Up until 1960, the uncontested leaders of the community were priests, and a few prominent businessmen involved in the transfer of workers and capital between Italy and Quebec.

But Italians were not entirely cut off from Quebec society. Even though they chose to live together in a few areas of the city, they still constituted minorities in neighbourhoods that were largely French-Canadian. They often had the same low standard of living as their French-Canadian neighbours. Because they were almost all Catholics, their children went to Catholic and usually French-language schools.[10] When they intermarried it was almost exclusively with French Canadians, rarely with English Canadians. Though the Italians maintained a separate cultural identity and strong sense of social cohesion until the Second World War, they did share with many French-Canadians a common socio-economic status and, to some extent, the use of the French language.[11]

The initial integration of Italians into Quebec life was coloured by two majors factors: the well-established pattern of separate ethnic institutions and the intense community life of the Italians. Both of these elements were profoundly affected by the new Quebec nationalism of the 1960s and by the new attitudes of post-war Italian immigrants.

As mentioned earlier, Italian immigration to Quebec began again during the 1950s after a twenty-year interruption. This second wave brought more Italians to Quebec than had come at the beginning of the century, some 60,000 during the 1950s. This meant that very soon the newcomers outnumbered the already established Italians and their children.

The new wave was not very different from the first. As a rule the newcomers came as part of a network based on kinship and neighbourhood. In Montreal they were met by relatives or friends, and their integration into the new city and milieu was relatively easy.

Despite these similarities, it did not take long for tensions to develop between the two groups, as Jeremy Boissevain noted as early as 1964-65. The older settlers had little education; they had come to Montreal during a period of economic uncertainty and hard work and had been severely affected by the difficulties of the Depression and the War. The newcomers were generally more educated and more dynamic; they were able to take advantage of post-war prosperity. During the 1950s there was a general rise in the standard of living in Montreal, and the situation of the Italians improved as well, even if they continued to hold low-skilled jobs in construction work and in factories. According to Boissevain, the differences between the two waves of immigrants provoked tensions within the community and tends to explain the new developments which manifested themselves in the community.[12]

The large number of newcomers changed the economic and cultural environment of the Italian community in Quebec. In one decade, the population increased from 34,165 to 108,552. The community now attained a critical mass which allowed it to support its own economic institutions. Numerous businesses sprang up, established by Italians and mainly employing Italians — the construction industry, for example, construction supplies and other kinds of industries and services. An ethnic economy, so to speak, came to exist within the larger economy of the city. Immigrants could work in a largely Italian milieu.[13]

Another important aspect of this growth was the emergence of a new group of wealthy businessmen, who quickly profited from the economic growth and accelerated urban development of the fifties and sixties. A few of these businessmen ran large firms which controlled veritable clienteles of employees and debtors — a new form of the *padronismo* of the beginning of the century.[14]

The new post-war conditions thus seemed to favour an even more cohesive structure within the Italian community and a strong sense of its cultural identity and separate existence as an ethnic group in Montreal. The Italians still tended to group together in the same residential areas, but this concentration was less marked than that of the Jews and the Greeks.[15]

Their isolation was reinforced by the new language choices which Italians made after the War. Until that time the majority of children of Italian origin studied in French in the Montreal Catholic school system. But gradually, more parents chose English and, by 1961, 70% of Italian children were attending schools in the English-Catholic system, which had been set up in the nineteenth century for the Irish population. In a way the Italians replaced the Irish, whose population had been in relative decline in Montreal since the end of the nineteenth century. The former Irish schools became English-language Italian schools. This change took place without any negative reactions on the part of French-Canadian leaders. Having opted for institutional isolationism, they made no effort to assimilate the immigrants or impose French on them or their children. In Montreal the anglicization of all those who were not French Canadians came to be considered normal.

The choice of English was totally logical for Italian immigrants. They left their country to improve their standard of living and to take advantage of North American economic prosperity. They saw upon arrival in Montreal that economic power spoke English and that the French Canadians were rarely able to get past the lower echelons in business. English seemed to be necessary for economic advancement and for mobility towards other areas of Canada and North America. But their choice of English as the language of instruction for their children by no means meant that Italian Montrealers became assimilated into the British community. Their most frequent contacts by far were with the French-Canadian community and they maintained a cultural identity which was their own.[16]

The New Quebec Nationalism

The strengthening of Italian identity began in the 1950s but it became especially evident during the 1960s with the spectacular outburst of a new form of Quebec nationalism on the part of the French-speaking population. This new nationalism radically challenged the historical compromise agreed to in the mid-nineteenth century and the regime of separate ethnic institutions it had created.[17]

This challenge resulted from the realization that, after a century of Confederation, French Canadians were still second-class citizens not only in Canada but especially within the very borders of Quebec where they made up 80% of the population. Their socio-economic status at the start of the 1960s was far lower than that of Anglo-Quebecers. Overall they were less educated, less skilled and held lower-level jobs. What is more, even educated and highly qualified French Canadians were as a group subject to discrimination. They had limited access to middle and high-level management positions and, given equal competence and training, their income was systematically lower than that of Anglo-Quebecers. This was shown conclusively in the studies of the Royal Commission on Bilingualism and Biculturalism.[18]

The nationalist reaction of the 1960s aimed first and foremost at correcting these inequalities by giving French Canadians an economic and social position consonant with their demographic importance, and by creating new structures in which they could develop freely. These goals supposed a thorough reform of French-Canadian society and its institutions. The spectacular reform of the educational system shows how eager French Canadians were to provide higher levels of schooling which were also better adapted to the needs of a modern society. The Quebec government became, for many people, the fundamental instrument of progress.

Correcting inequalities also meant challenging the historical privileges of the British minority. Although their demographic weight had been declining for several years, their economic power was still very strong everywhere in Quebec and was especially evident in Montreal.

In the first stage of reform, during the better part of the 1960s, there was no thought of eliminating either separate ethnic institutions as such or anglophone cultural institutions. Quebec's new political and intellectual leaders aimed simply at redressing the balance, by strengthening the role of the State, making it serve francophones more openly and giving it the task of ensuring that all the peoples of Quebec had equal opportunities and increased access to education, health and social services.

During the 1960s, however, the new Quebec nationalism became more complex, dividing itself into moderate and radical tendencies. The gradual rise of the independence movement represented first by the *Rassemblement pour l'indépendance nationale* and then by the *Parti québécois*, accentuated this radicalization. Soon, it was no longer equality of opportunity which was being demanded but a transformation of society so that it might become more clearly French-speaking. More and more intellectuals and a number of politicians demanded that Quebec become as French as Ontario was English. They rejected traditional bilingualism, which they said would lead only to assimilation; they argued instead for making society and its institutions French-speaking.

On the question of ethnic relations, the independence type of nationalism was expansionist and even imperialist. The rejection of assimilation which had been the hallmark of ethnic relations since the middle of the nineteenth century was totally discarded. Strategies of integration and linguistic assimilation were now advocated, strategies of a melting pot *à la québécoise*. The most radical nationalists even openly invited Anglo-Quebecers to choose between becoming French or leaving the province. Governments obviously did not go that far, but the tone was set and undeniably the old compromise was shaken.[19]

It is important here to distinguish between nationalism and independence. Quebec nationalism is a far-reaching phenomenon, with deep historical roots and real links with the popular classes of Quebec. Independence is only one way of expressing nationalism; it obtained the support of a very vocal minority of intellectuals, artists and what we might call a new middle class which was associated with public sector institutions.

Quebec governments have always defended nationalist positions, although to differing degrees. Since the beginning of the century at least, Quebec prime ministers have acted as spokespersons for French Canadians within Confederation. This role was strengthened during the sixties and seventies. All the successive Quebec governments — from the Liberals of Jean Lesage, to the *Union nationale* of Daniel Johnson and Jean-Jacques Bertrand, to the Liberals again under Robert Bourassa, and to the *Parti québécois* of René Lévesque — defended nationalist positions which expressed the same determination to make Quebec and its institutions more French-speaking. Where each government differed was in the means which it proposed.

Ethnic groups not defined as either anglophone or francophone seemed at first to be outsiders in the debate. They were soon drawn into it, however. Anglo-Quebec leaders quickly saw that the integration of allophone ethnic communities into the English-language school system would strengthen the British minority whose numbers were in relative decline. They saw that it was in their interest to forget the discriminatory attitudes of the past and to accept the transformation of the Anglo-Protestant and Anglo-Catholic school systems into English-language multi-ethnic systems. That way they could preserve and strengthen their own institutions, at least in Montreal.

For their part, the French-speaking community had always counted on the strength of numbers. With the dramatic drop in the French-Canadian birthrate at the end of the sixties, this strength was increasingly fragile. Many analysts and intellectuals realized that the future growth of the Quebec population would depend on immigration and that in the medium term the proportion of French Canadians in Quebec might decrease.[20]

For many observers, the future of French Quebec depended on making the allophones French speaking and it became essential that immigrants join the francophone group. Two complementary strategies were envisaged. The first consisted in attempting to modify immigration patterns by recruiting immigrants principally from French-speaking countries. A number of measures were taken by the end of the 1960s towards this objective, in particular the creation of the Quebec Ministry of Immigration. But this reorientation came about at a time when the overall rate of immigration to Quebec was considerably reduced. So soon after this, strategists turned to the second option — that of making immigrants already settled in Quebec and especially their children French-speaking. The language battle had begun.

The Language Battle

The Italians of Quebec were at the centre of this battle for several reasons. First, as we have seen, they were the largest ethnic group after the French and the British. Their numbers, their visibility, and their geographic concentration made them the symbol of all the allophone groups. What is more, the many immigrants among them were perceived as less acculturated to the British group than the Ashkenazy Jews, for example. In addition, French Canadians traditionally had closer contacts with the Italians of Quebec. The fact that most Italians chose to attend English schools was a recent phenomenon which marked a break with the past. Many French Canadians were shocked when they learned how many Italians preferred English schools. There had also been something of an aggressive side.to relations between French Canadians and Italians among the lower classes because the two groups competed in the same job market. Through their community structures Italians were organized and had leaders able to engage in public debate — in French — with French Canadians.

The language battle began in 1968 in Saint-Leonard, a new Montreal suburb whose population was then mainly French Canadian but with a very strong minority of Italian origin. The Saint-Leonard conflict, however, was just the spark which led to a heightened awareness of the importance of linguistic questions and of the language of instruction for all ethnic groups in Quebec.

Italians had their own positions to defend. They entered the debate on the basis of what they considered to be their own interests and they became important participants in it. But it must be recognized that Italians also became pawns in a battle between French and English Canadians and that they were used in a conflict which was not necessarily their own.

Beginning in 1968 Quebec governments, under pressure from francophone groups, brought in legislation to regulate language use in Quebec. At first, this intervention concerned the language of instruction only, but gradually the objective became the making of all areas of society French-speaking.

Before 1968 the language of instruction was determined by what was called free choice. Whatever their ethnic origins, parents could choose to send their children to French or English schools, the only criterion being religion. Catholics, whether English or French-speaking, were served by the Catholic system. All the others used the Protestant system which was overwhelmingly English, although there were a few French schools.

The first legislative act, Bill 63, was passed in 1968. It sanctioned the existing principle of free choice but sought to promote the teaching of French in the English school system and to ensure that all the peoples of Quebec, whatever their origin, be able to speak French. Because it maintained the principle of free choice, Bill 63 was received with indignation by many francophone nationalist groups. Their opposition contributed to the fall of the *Union nationale* government which passed the law.

Following the report of the Gendron Commission on the status of French in Quebec, the Liberal government adopted Bill 22 in 1974 which went much further in establishing the priority of French in Quebec society. It made an important new change concerning the language of instruction: the English system was to remain intact for the population of British origin, but immigrant children were to enter the French school system. Only those who could pass a test proving competence in English were allowed to enter English schools: all the others were obliged to register in French schools. Bill 22 was intended to increase the prestige of the French language and extend its use to all sectors of activity. The act was greeted with cries of protest not only by anglophone groups, traditional supporters of the Liberals, but also by the Italian community which was directly affected. It also received negative reactions from the most nationalist francophone groups and from those favouring independence, who considered that it did not go far enough.

In 1976, as soon as it came into power, the *Parti québécois* government began preparations for a new law, Bill 101, called the "Charter of the French language," which was passed in 1977. It strengthened measures already provided for in Bill 22, considerably restricting access to English-language schools. Only children with at least one parent who had studied in an English-language primary school in Quebec were allowed to attend. It also added greater rigour and compulsion to measures in Bill 22 dealing with the making of Quebec society French-speaking. The intention of the Charter of the French language was not only to give schools and other public institutions a French character, but to make the entire society French-speaking.[21]

As a result of the many changes which occurred between 1968 and 1977, the management of ethnic relations was entirely transformed, particularly with respect to language issues. The Quebec State openly became the government of French Canadians and implemented a number of measures intended to make English less attractive to both allophones and some francophones. In the period of a few short years, the rules of the game had changed completely.

How did Italians react to these changes? It is important here not to overgeneralize. Just as francophone nationalism had different tendencies, the reactions of the Italian community were diverse. The media only presented the most extreme positions. While there was clearly a majority tendency within the Italian population, there was also a diversity of positions.

The Italian community of Montreal had never been

perfectly united. It had always been marked by the tensions and oppositions that are normal in any group of that size. From the early years, there existed regional divisions. More recently there was the distinction between older and newer immigrants.[22] Language choices also created separations: those who studied in French became integrated into different networks from their compatriots educated in English.[23] Social milieux, business interests, political options were also divisive factors. In fact the social and political geography of the Italian community has yet to be defined and studied.

It is clear nonetheless that a majority of Italians reacted very negatively to the language laws. These laws jeopardized the choices they had made for their children and changed their perceptions of Quebec and Canadian society.

Some chose open resistance: rejection of the policy of "francisation," organization of clandestine classes, illegal registration of children in English schools. This resistance was led by the *Consiglio educativo italo-canadese*. It was actively supported by the English-language press and by the administrators and teachers of the Anglo-Catholic school system.

Other leaders opted for negotiation and conciliation. Some tried to get concessions through the political parties. They put their hopes in the Liberals and felt deceived by Bill 22. In 1976 they fell back on the *Union nationale* and in 1981 turned again to the Liberal Party.

My intention here is not to trace all the events which marked the opposition of numerous Italian-speaking groups to the language laws, but to stress certain aspects of the way in which these events were interpreted.[24]

Except for a few extremist groups, the majority of Italian leaders did not officially object to the increased use of French in Quebec. They were however opposed to unilingualism and favoured the idea of a bilingual Quebec. This stand made them supporters of the federal Liberal anti-nationalist position of Pierre Elliot Trudeau and opponents of nationalist Liberals and advocates of independence.

The majority of Italians were for the status quo — free choice — which in practice meant the right to educate their children in English. They were convinced that English was essential for socio-economic advancement and necessary to ensure that their children could move out of Quebec if they wished.

There is another aspect to the Italian reaction that many French-speaking analysts tend to neglect but which from the Italian point of view was absolutely fundamental. Spokespersons for Italian organizations considered that the language laws were discriminatory because they protected the acquired educational rights of Anglo-Quebecers but neglected those of immigrants by making French obligatory for children of immigrants. The following argument was heard on several occasions: if you wish to make the school system French, impose French on everyone, even Anglo-Quebecers; then we will accept it as well.

These arguments had no effect on Quebec governments. Italian and other opposition groups representing ethnic minorities are now trying out a new strategy: they are using the new Canadian constitution, which was imposed on Quebec in 1981, and its Charter of Rights, to contest the constitutionality of the Quebec language laws in court.

The language battle has been going on now for about twenty years and it is perhaps time to examine its results.

What were its effects for Quebec society as a whole and for the Italian community in Montreal? Who has gained from the conflict?

Italians and a Decade of Change in Quebec 1970-1980

Beyond the conflicts and the language question itself, Quebec has become undeniably more French since 1960 and this process was accelerated in the second half of the 1970s. The political will of successive governments and the laws adopted certainly contributed to this process, but it is important to recognize that these laws expressed a much larger social fact.

A new generation of more educated French Canadians emerged during this period who were better able to demand their place in the sun; they wanted to see an end to centuries-old discriminatory practices against French Canadians.

Members of this generation took advantage first of the rapid growth in the public sector, especially in education, medical and social services, and in the government administration. They were given positions of responsibility which were still hard to obtain in the private sector.

This trend spread during the 1970s to the private sector. The decade saw the emergence of new large-scale enterprises under francophone control. Anglophone businesses became conscious of the need to make their activities operate in French in Quebec and to open their doors to francophone executives. But many of these businesses, especially large pan-Canadian and international firms, moved their head offices to Toronto. While these moves might have been accelerated by the language debates, their real cause was fundamentally economic. The centre of economic activity in Canada has been moving since the beginning of the century and in recent years Toronto has taken over from Montreal as the metropolis of Canada. The moves of head offices caused thousands of Anglo-Quebec executives who occupied management positions in these firms to go to Ontario. English-speaking university graduates saw that job opportunities were shrinking in Quebec but expanding in Toronto and in the West, and they also left in large numbers.

Montreal lost many head offices but retained regional operations which functioned more and more in French. At the beginning of the 1980s the language situation in the private sector in Quebec was very different from what had prevailed ten years earlier. For example, some large Anglo-Canadian banks now have francophone vice-presidents heading their Quebec activities, a situation which would have been unthinkable in the mid-1960s. These changes therefore contributed to the intensified French character of Quebec.

What has happened to the Italians in all this? Have the options of the last four decades led them to an impasse? The young Italian children who received an English education in view of a job market which in the 1960s was strongly English now find themselves in a society where the job market has become to a large extent French-speaking.

Will they tend to fall back on the separate ethnic institutions of the past? We have seen that their language choices were never apparently intended as a step towards cultural assimilation with the larger groups. On the contrary, recent language tensions seem to have had the effect of strengthening the Italian sense of identity in Montreal. Italian is used much more for family and neighbourhood communication than it is in Toronto, for instance. The tensions resulted in a new political awareness, the emergence of a new leadership and the creation of new organizations, in particular the *Congrès national des Italo-Canadiens (Québec)*. The system of separate institutions became even stronger.

According to sociologists Claude Painchaud and Richard Poulin, these developments worked primarily to the advantage of the new Italian bourgeoisie, which arose out of the ethnic economy and the Italian labour market. These businessmen succeeded in replacing the old elites and took over the leadership of the official organizations of the Italian community. According to Painchaud and Poulin, the ethnic and language tensions of those years allowed a new Italian-Quebec bourgeoisie to establish power within the community.

Perhaps the developments of the last few years have accentuated the "ghettoization" of the Italians. But it is possible to imagine the beginnings of a medium-term solution: a process which would put an end to ethnic isolation without imposing assimilation or denying cultural specificity. Such tendencies have surfaced over the last few years. When their phase of linguistic imperialism ended in the late 1970s, supporters of the independence option began to show more openness toward the ethnic and cultural diversity of Quebec. *Cultural communities* is now the term used; a Ministry has been created and it promotes programmes to teach heritage languages. The idea of a melting pot *à la québécoise* is losing ground. Academics are falling into step: research on ethnic groups is now one of the most dynamic fields in the Quebec social sciences.

As for the Italians, they too are undergoing changes. A recent study shows more acceptance of the French fact.

Although they still wish to maintain their cultural autonomy, a growing number of Italian intellectuals are seeking stronger links with francophones.

These trends are part of a long-term historical process, however; and while certain tendencies are visible, it is too soon to come to firm conclusions on the future orientation of Quebec society.

* * *

Italians have been at the centre of an important political and language debate in Quebec over the last two decades. To understand these recent developments, we had to look at the long history of ethnic relations to which they belong. History obviously cannot explain everything, but it can provide important insight for an understanding of the present.

The Italian community of Quebec took root and developed within the system of separate ethnic institutions which was established during the nineteenth century by French and English Canadians. Faced with the ethnic isolation imposed by the receiving society, Italians created an intense community life. These structures allowed them to find their own solutions to economic difficulty, distrust and discrimination which are the lot of all immigrants.

The nationalist challenge to the traditional system of ethnic relations in the 1960s resulted in a strengthening of Italian community identity and of its "ghettoisation." It also gave rise to strong tensions and deep misunderstandings between French Canadians and Italians in Montreal.

We are now on the threshold of a new era in the history of Quebec. The two communities must develop new, more open means of communication and a path to mutual acceptance. This is the challenge of the future, the history of a future which has yet to be written.

NOTES

1. See among others, Jeremy Boissevain, *The Italians of Montreal: Social Adjustment in a Plural Society* (Ottawa, 1971); Mauro F. Malservisi, *La contribution des groupes ethniques autres que français et britannique au développement du Québec* (Québec, 1973); "Enjeux ethniques. Production de nouveaux rapports sociaux," special issue of *Sociologie et sociétés* XV, 2 (octobre 1983); "Migrations et communautés culturelles," spécial issue of *Questions de culture* 2 (1982).

2. Hubert Charbonneau, ed., *La population du Québec: études rétrospectives* (Montréal, 1973); Helen I. Cowan, *British Emigration to British North America* (Toronto, 1961); Paul-André Linteau, "La montée du cosmopolitisme montréalais," *Questions de culture* 2(1982), 23-27.

3. Paul-André Linteau, René Durocher and Jean-Claude Robert, *Quebec: A History, 1867-1929* (Toronto, 1983), 18-54.

4. *Ibid.*

5. Paul-André Linteau, "La montée du cosmopolitisme montréalais," 27-42. The ten-year censuses of the Canadian population undertaken since 1851 are the main source for the compilation of the populations of the ethnic groups. See also Ronald Rudin, *The Forgotten Quebecers: A History of English-Speaking Quebec 1759-1980* (Quebec, 1985).

6. Hubert Charbonneau et Robert Maheu, *Les aspects démographiques de la question linguistique* (synthèse pour la Commission d'enquête sur la situation de la langue française et sur les droits linguistiques au Québec, Québec, 1973); Claude Painchaud et Richard Poulin, "L'Italianité, conflit linguistique et structure du pouvoir dans la communauté italo-québécoise," *Sociologie et sociétés* XV, 2 (octobre 1983), 89-93; Linteau, "La montée du cosmopolitisme montréalais," 42-48.

7. Michel Laferrière, "L'éducation des enfants des groupes minoritaires au Québec: de la définition par les groupes eux-mêmes à l'intervention de l'État," *Sociologie et sociétés* XV, 2 (octobre 1983), 120-23.

8. See the remarks in Mauro F. Malservisi, *La contribution des groupes ethniques*, chap. 5.

9. Bruno Ramirez, *Les premiers Italiens de Montréal. L'origine de la Petite Italie du Québec* (Montréal, 1984). This book is a revised and expanded version of an earlier booklet: *The Italians of Montreal: From Sojourning to Settlement, 1900-1921* (Montreal, 1980). See also "Montreal's Italians and the Socioeconomy of Settlement, 1900-1930: Some Historical Hypotheses," *Urban History Review/Revue d'histoire urbaine* IX, 1 (juin 1981), 39-48; Sylvie Taschereau, "Pays et patries: mariages et lieux d'origine des Italiens de Montréal, 1906-1930" (M.A. thesis, History, Université du Québec à Montréal, 1984).

10. In the beginning the Italian community set up separate schools which provided some instruction in Italian; they were gradually integrated into the Catholic School Commission of Montreal. Michel Laferrière, "L'éducation des enfants...," 121. On the development of the Italian-Quebec school issue, see Donat Taddeo and Ray-

mond Tarras, *Le débat linguistique au Québec: la communauté italienne et la langue d'enseignement* (Montréal, 1987).

11. See Charles Baily, "The Social Structure of the Italian and Ukrainian Immigrant Communities in Montreal, 1935-37" (M.A. thesis, Sociology, McGill University, 1939); Taschereau, *Pays et patries...*

12. Boissevain, *The Italians of Montreal*, 28-32.

13. Painchaud et Poulin, "L'Italianité...," 96-97.

14. On "padronismo," see Ramirez, *Les premiers Italiens*, 46-55; Robert Harney, "Montreal's King of Italian Labour: A Case Study of Padronism," *Labour/Le travailleur* 4 (1979), 57-84.

15. Mario Polèse, Charles Hamel et Antoine Bailly, *La géographie résidentielle des immigrants et des groupes ethniques: Montréal, 1971* (Montréal, 1978).

16. Boissevain, *The Italians of Montreal*; Painchaud et Poulin, "Italianité...."

17. On the important changes occurring during this period, see P.A. Linteau, R. Durocher, J.-C. Robert and F. Ricard, *Histoire du Québec contemporain*. Tome 2. *Le Québec depuis 1930* (Montréal, 1986), 739 p.

18. *Report of the Royal Commission on Bilingualism and Biculturalism*, Vol. 3 (Ottawa, 1964); Lysiane Gagnon, "Les conclusions du Rapport B.B.: De Durham à Laurendeau-Dunton: variations sur le thème de la dualité canadienne," *Économie québécoise* (Québec, 1969), 233-52.

19. Guy Bouthillier et Jean Meynaud, *Le Choc des langues au Québec 1760-1970* (Montréal, 1972).

20. Hubert Charbonneau, Jacques Henripin et Jacques Légaré, "L'avenir démographique des francophones au Québec et à Montréal en l'absence de politiques adéquates," *Revue de géographie de Montréal* XXIV, 2 (1970), 199-202.

21. See Denise Daoust, "La planification linguistique au Québec: un aperçu des lois sur la langue," *Revue québécoise de linguistique* 12, 1(1982), 9-75; Raymond Breton et Gail Grant, *La langue de travail au Québec* (Montréal, 1981), 7-24.

22. Boissevain, *Les Italiens de Montréal*, 28-32.

23. Interview with Antoine Del Busso, April 1984.

24. Claude Painchaud et Richard Poulin, "Les Italiens au Québec. Histoire et sociologie d'une communauté" (manuscript), chap. 8; D. Taddeo et R. Tarras, *Le débat linguistique au Québec.*

Contemporary Italo-Canadian Literature

Susan Iannucci

Italo-Canadian literature fits into the larger context of Canadian literature, and Canadian literature starts in the wilderness, in the bush. The very earliest texts we have are the journals written by explorers like Samuel Hearne and Alexander Mackenzie, or the reports made by missionaries. These people recorded their observations of and reactions to the vast land in which they found themselves. They were people who had come from somewhere else, from Europe, for specific purposes: to explore or to convert. They brought with them a series of cultural assumptions, of stock responses, which had been formed back home.

Their vocabulary and their notions about social hierarchy simply were not equal to the realities they encountered in the New World. A good example is Susanna Moodie. Best remembered for her journal, *Roughing It in the Bush*, Susanna Moodie was quite simply appalled by some of the people who considered themselves her social and intellectual equals.[1] Yet, like later immigrants, she did slowly adapt to the customs and necessities of the New World. In the eight years covered in *Roughing It in the Bush*, she abandoned her imported notions of social hierarchy and gained a sense of where her real superiority lay.

Roughing It in the Bush is a forerunner of the first text in Italian-Canadian literature, Mario Duliani's *La ville sans femmes.*[2] Duliani was a journalist by profession, and *La ville sans femmes* is the first account by a professional writer of Italian origin to detail the experience of Italian Canadians in Canada. It is striking how much it has in common with *Roughing It in the Bush*, despite the fact that it was published almost one hundred years later.

Both books have a thesis. *Roughing It in the Bush* ends with the words:

> If these sketches should prove the means of deterring one family from sinking their property, and shipwrecking all their hopes, by going to reside in the backwoods of Canada, I shall consider myself amply repaid for revealing the secrets of the prison-house, and feel that I have not toiled and suffered in the wilderness in vain.[3]

A "prison-house" she calls it. She is speaking metaphorically, of course. On the other hand, Mario Duliani's prison was a real one. "La ville sans femmes" was an internment camp, and the book Duliani wrote about it is what he calls a *reportage romancé*, a fictionalized account of the forty months he spent in two different camps during World War II. Like Susanna Moodie, Mario Duliani finds himself in the middle of the wilderness, although bars on the windows and a fence of barbed wire around the perimeter of the camp reinforce his isolation. He speaks over and over again of his sense of being "enseveli dans la forêt"[4] [entombed in the forest] while Moody says, "it is as if the grave had closed over you, and the hearts that once knew and loved you know you no more." Life in the prison-house is not life at all.

If Moodie's purpose is to warn off potential emigrants to the "prison-house," Duliani's is to pour fulsome praise on the prison camps he spent so long in. There is, of course a reason for what seems at first an odd approach to his subject. *La ville sans femmes*, published in 1945, is a self-vindication, a public act of Canadian patriotism, which is to set him straight forever with the authorities.

I have dwelt on this text because it seems to me that it makes clear the connection between early Italian-Canadian literature and other early Canadian literature. French-Canadian novels like Louis Hémon's *Maria Chapdelaine* or Ringuet's *Thirty Acres* illustrate this too. The point is that the nineteenth-century immigrant like Susanna Moodie has a parallel in the twentieth-century immigrant Mario Duliani. Both find themselves in a forest which they try to turn into a garden; both are cut off from a culture where they had a place and thrust into one where they do not feel at home; both talk frequently about disease and feel like they have vanished into the grave; finally, both are imprisoned. This image of imprisonment is an important one. It is related to another image out of our historical past, the garrison, and in later Italo-Canadian literature it transmutes into Little Italy. The barbed wire of Duliani's account disappears. The new barriers are linguistic and cultural, but the isolation is just as real.

Little Italy is not just an historical phenomenon but also a psychological one. It is the imaginative presence a poet like Joseph Pivato can conjure up simply by naming "*doferin e san cler*" — he uses a phonetic spelling to elicit from the reader the Italianized pronunciation — in a poem entitled ironically "Cultura Canadese."[5] The impulse to create a Little Italy grows out of a need to recreate home. As long as the immigrant stays within its confines, he does not have to adapt to the surrounding, "foreign" culture.

In a 1978 interview with Celestino De Iuliis, the Toronto poet Pier Giorgio Di Cicco commented on the psychological impact an Italian immigrant community as large as the one in Toronto has on its members. He said:

> Here in Toronto there is an ingrownness, there is an unwillingness to move out, a centripetal force pulling us back into the family, back into the community itself.[6]

In Di Cicco's view there is a reactionary force at work in Toronto trying to keep the second generation (like him) firmly behind the cultural barriers with the first. It is interesting that he identifies the family as one of the manifestations of Little Italy, for it is in this guise that it turns up most frequently in contemporary Italo-Canadian writing.

The publication in 1978 of *Roman Candles*, an anthology of seventeen Italo-Canadian poets edited by Di Cicco, was an important event. It was the first collection of purely Italo-Canadian poetry, and it helped to focus attention on this kind of writing as a cultural phenomenon. A cursory glance at the Table of Contents reveals at least three poets who are moved to call poems "The Immigrant" or variations thereon. Many more write about the experience of immigration, and the effects on them of being raised in Canada by parents who were raised somewhere else.

In part, this concentration on *italianità* is a function of the mood of the editor as he put together the anthology. He was looking for Italo-Canadian poets, and he chose the most Italian of these Canadian poets' work for the volume.

These poets are the second generation, the children of immigrants. Some were born in Italy and brought to North America at a young age, but many were born here. It is they who are doing the writing, because theirs is the first generation to have the leisure to write, as well as the words. In his Preface, Di Cicco says of them (*RC*, pp. 9-10):

> They are in the fortunate and tragic position of having to live with two cultures, one more exterior than the other. They will find it harder to go back to Italy than their parents did. They belong and do not belong. This tension is at the centre of their poetry, and is in some cases the impetus behind it.

Actually, these Italo-Canadian writers carry a dual burden. If they have interpreted the outside community to their families while growing up, as writers they also interpret their Italo-Canadian inheritance to their readers. Mediation is a two-way street.

A recurring theme in *Roman Candles* is the return visit to Italy of the second-generation poet, and his registration of his reactions to that experience. Most return to small towns buried in Calabria, Sicily, or Friuli where the cycle of life still follows the cycle of the seasons. The structures are archaic; history has passed them by, like the *autostrada del sole*, on the way to somewhere else. The advantage of such a life, of course, is that the village holds a place for everyone, including the aged, infirm, or mentally deficient, and everyone knows what that place is. Tony Pignataro writes (*RC*, pp. 48-9):

> The order of their lives was simple.
> The meaning of their existence profound.
> Events cyclical. Birth and death; for one there
> was a reason, for the other a necessity....
>
> *A man's work, the seed pouch girdled to his waist. A pointed stick to open earth. And after the harvest the feel of hands like tree bark or eroded stones. This is legacy; a man's years at the plough. This you can leave to your children with pride, renewal, lambs in the spring, seasonal toil.*

This is the world Tony Pignataro has lost. His memory holds a pastoral vision of a golden age with things like the cold of winter, backbreaking labour, crop failures, and children dying in infancy left out. But as we all know, it is vision which shapes reality. Pignataro has lost the sense of belonging to a never-ending cycle, with his place in the cycle clearly defined. In his radical dislocation, he has been deprived of this sense of continuity, of building anew on foundations laid by other men (*RC*, p. 50):

> So rich with ruins
> is the land
> that when a man decides
> to build a house, he has simply

to find traces of an old foundation,
  clear the débris
and build on it or beside it.

  This is the inheritance of sons;
to be rooted in their father's faith.
To rediscover hewn stone.

Other second-generation immigrants return to their country of origin with more complex burdens. Di Cicco himself is one such poet. The trip to Arezzo in 1974 which culminated in the anthology *Roman Candles* forced him to confront in person the country he knew essentially only through his parents' stories. He had a lot of ghosts to exorcize and, in addition, he was motivated by the child's need to verify his parents' accounts of his past.

In his search for concrete images of that past, Di Cicco is attracted particularly by the bar in the railway station in Arezzo. The poem is called "Memento d'Italia" (*RC*, p. 34). Here Di Cicco glimpses what Arezzo must have been like before the massive destruction it underwent in World War II. He is trying to reach past the trauma his parents suffered to images of ordinary life, and he succeeds. He finds the vivid sensory impressions he needs to make his parents' past real to him. From other poems (notably "The Man Called Beppino," p. 31) we know of his father's disillusionment with the land of his dreams and of his early death. We also know of the respect and affection in which his son holds his memory. These charge with poignancy the former poem's restrained last line, "Much that went between this man and I is changed" (p. 35).

The return to Italy, in the flesh or in the imagination,

also inspires prose writers. C.D. Minni's short story "Roots" is about a construction worker's return, with his Canadian-born wife and children, after an absence of twenty years, to the town in Calabria where he was born. As Minni presents it, his character's purpose is to reunite his present self, the face he sees in the mirror, with the younger self that emigrated so long ago. In his hometown he meets a friend who says:

> "I knew you'd return.... They always do, like our swallows. But not to stay?"

And he replies, "My roots are in Canada." The rest of the story disperses any lingering doubts he may entertain on the subject. At the end he is sitting in a cafe sipping local wine and savouring the experience. The return has taught him where home lies:

> Not bad, I think, drinking Gran Caruso. Not bad at all, but it is not me.[7]

The second generation often labours under a considerable burden of anxiety. It is, to borrow an image from the Toronto poet Mary Di Michele, "caught/with one bare foot in a village in the Abruzzi,/ the other busy with cramped English speaking toes in Toronto" (*RC*, p. 62). The writers of this generation retain a strong sense of the values that have motivated their parents' emigration and many sacrifices. At the same time, some are wracked by guilt because they cannot accept their parents' expectations and way of life. They cannot accept the values of Little Italy, embodied as Di Cicco says in the family. At the same time, they find it hard to hack a different path through the wilderness for themselves. This duality finds expression in the literature in various ways. Mary Di Michele's prize-winning poem, "Mimosa," sets a Martha and Mary dichotomy between two sisters against a portrait of their defeated, brooding Italian immigrant father. None of the three is happy. Marta, the loyal stay-at-home daughter, claims to have spent her entire life trying to please her father in classic Martha fashion. In fact, her self-denial masks selfishness. Her lengthy and angry apologia ends with the petulant complaint:

> I only want my fair share.
> I want what's mine and what Lucia kicks over.
> I want father to stop mooning about her
> and listen to my rendition of Mimosa.[8]

The repeated "I want" makes it clear that her voluntary self-sequestration within the walls of her parents' expectations had only made her bitter.

On the other hand, Lucia, despite her apparent rebellion, is truly loyal. She begins by saying, "So much of my life has been wasted feeling guilty/about disappointing my father and mother." Yet her forays beyond the walls of their experience, so strongly frowned upon by her parents and so costly to her in terms of peace of mind, have filled her with love and understanding. Her final words show deep affection for her father and a loving appreciation of how much they have in common:

> I have his face, his eyes, his hands,
> his anxious desire to know everything,
> to think, to write everything,
> his anxious desire to be heard,

and we love each other and say nothing,
we love each other in that country
we couldn't live in.[9]

In contrast to her sister's diction, Lucia's is full of third person singular and first person plural pronouns. Her guilt and her suffering have taught her how to love, something her sister has never learned.

This sense of guilt towards parents shows up in other poets too. It is part of the dilemma of the second generation. They are fully aware of what their parents gave up for them, but at times their own sense of loss, of belonging to neither the Old World nor the New, is so strong that they are not the least bit grateful for what was done on their behalf but without their consent. In one of Saro D'Agostino's "Immigrant Songs," which picks up the image of the prison (*RC*, p. 71), the poet-persona feels simultaneously responsible for his father's pain and incapable of alleviating it. Saro D'Agostino has built his own prison, or perhaps the society beyond the walls has forced him into it. The underlying irony is that his voice has carried beyond the prison walls; the songs for which he apologizes are actually his salvation.

Of the longer works, Frank Paci's three novels, *The Italians, Black Madonna*, and *The Father* all explore the intricacies of relations between the first and second generations and the attempts (or refusal to try) of each generation to adapt to the surrounding community.[10] Marco Micone's play *Gens du silence*[11] traces the exploitation of Italian immigrants, particularly the women, both at home and in the factory while Filippo Salvatore's screen play *La Fresque de Mussolini*[12] looks at the plight of Italian immigrant workers in the Montreal of Camillien Houde and Maurice

Duplessis at the moment when Mussolini invaded Ethiopia.

One indication of how assimilation is proceeding has to do with names. What you call yourself indicates how you see yourself and how you want others to think of you. This is a passage from Frank Paci's novel, *The Father*:

> On his first day at high school his homeroom teacher, Father Kiley... asked him what he'd like to be called: Stefano or Stephen. He had written Stefano in the box with his large stilted hand. But when asked the question it suddenly dawned on him that he had a choice — and choosing gave him a great sense of satisfaction.
>
> From now on he was going to be Stephen.[13]

Since names are bound up with identity, nothing could express the dualism of belonging to two cultures better than a character with two names. More serious, however, is the cultural imperialism which simply takes over characters, including historical personages, and changes their names to forms it can pronounce. Filippo Salvatore wonders at this tendency in an oft-quoted poem (*RC*, p. 14):

> Giovanni, they erected you a monument,
> but they changed your name; here
> they call you John. And you
> look at them from your stony
> pedestal with a hardly perceivable
> grin on your bronze lips.

Salvatore is standing in a park in Montreal addressing a bronze statue of the man English-speaking Canadians call "John Cabot."

Related to the issue of names and naming is that of stereotyping. In *Roman Candles* there is a pair of matched poems about grandfathers, the second a refutation of the first. The first poem is by Len Gasparini and it is called "The Photograph of My Grandfather Reading Dante" (*RC*, p. 28).

> Every evening
> he would sit for hours
> in his favorite old rocking chair,
> holding a glass of homemade wine,
> with the *Divina Commedia* in his lap
> and a snuff box on the table beside him....
>
> And while the rest of our family played
> cards or listened to Italian music,
> I would study his wrinkled, serene
> face and love him. He was once
> photographed without
> even knowing it.

Caro Cantasano's poem, which is printed alongside it in *Roman Candles*, rejects what Cantasano sees as a fake appeal to a nonexistent cultural past. It is called simply "My Grandfather Didn't" (*RC*, p. 29).

> My grandfather didn't
> read Dante
> in a rocking chair me
> at his feet....
>
> * * *
>
> He could draw, tell stories, intaglio a specialty
> but no Dante
> just a name

instead he read the draft
for war in Lybia....

* * *

Grandfathers read Dante
in poems
fake memories mongering
culture....

Mine swore
"Cazzu 'mu ti futti!"

Nonno was a man of pierced ears.

Gasparini is interested in the stereotypes which are attached to people of Italian origin, as he demonstrates in other poems. There is in *Roman Candles* a poem which is a tribute to Giorgio Di Cicco, called "Il Sangue" (*RC*, p. 26-7). It is a protest against the kind of narrow-mindedness that reduces individuals to stereotypes. Surprisingly, its tone is not bitter; Gasparini accepts the stereotype "Italians are bricklayers" and turns it into a metaphor for creative activity. Hence the poem is as much about poetics as it is about stereotyping. Finally, Gasparini is the author of a wonderful poem which sends up the whole business of Italian stereotypes. It takes the Mafia as the source of its imagery, and uses it to ridicule everything in sight, with the profession of the poet at the top of the list. It is called "I Was a Poet for the Mafia" (*RC*, pp. 24-5).

This playful send-up of poetic activity brings us back to a more serious theme in Italian-Canadian literature: death. It arises naturally out of the Italo-Canadian writer's concentration on relationships within the family, and it almost always signals the death of a culture or a way of life. One of the tragedies of immigration is that usually one is not at hand when one's parents die back home. Antonino Mazza records the heartsickness of the bereaved family in Canada in a poem called "Death in Italy" (*RC*, pp. 40-1).

> Death for us is God's unjust jest
> we don't so much question its necessity
> but are enraged by His intrusion in our harmony
>
> It wasn't the first time that before God's
> wrath my father had shown his capacity
> for insanity but this time he was here and
> death was in Italy
>
> Ah, not to have seen one's father die!
> And yet you'd think he'd find comforting
> that he'd been a dutiful son that before he
> came away he'd built a chapel for his parents
> in the town's Holyground
> that he'd named his first born to carry on
> his father's good name.
>
> * * *
>
> Ah God, are they not our families, without
> a place to go back to what will be our lives!
>
> If I turn to their sighs it's because I can't find
> the words to describe what in time of crisis
> creeps inside their minds.

As this poem makes clear, one of the things that helps preserve the immigrant's equilibrium in his new land is the older generation back home. The immigrant is, as it were, suspended between his parents, left behind when he emigrated, and his children, busily going to school in Canada. When the elderly parents do eventually die, the balance alters. If there has been any doubt in his mind, this is the moment at which the immigrant realizes that his future lies in Canada. He gives up the notion he may have entertained vaguely for years of returning some day to the town where he was born and buying a vineyard, as the sojourners of his grandparents' generation did.

If it is hard to bear the death of close relatives in faraway lands, it is equally hard to die far from the land where you were born, and not be buried in the family vault. Frank Paci's novel *Black Madonna* is framed by two such deaths. First Adamo — the "first man" — worn out by a lifetime of physical labour in the steel plant, dies. Then, at the end of the novel Assunta, his wife, who has never ventured outside the confines of house and family, is hit by a train when she wanders onto the railway tracks in a state of distraction. It is ironic that the pair of deaths serve to reattach the oldest child, Marie, to the Italian past preserved for her in the form of photographs and a dowry chest brought by her mother from Italy. The novel ends with Marie boarding a plane to take the chest back to Italy to give as a wedding present to the real inheritor of the tradition it represents, her cousin Marisa.

The photograph, in fact, is a good image both of and for the vanished past because it is static. When an immigrant leaves his home, he takes with him a mental impression, a mental photograph, if you will, of what that home looks like at the moment of his departure. As the years pass, that mental picture, like the physical one, does not change. The immigrant does not see the new houses built near the monument, the Fiat plant outside town, the new priest. For him, life in the village is still the way it was at the moment he left, and its customs live on in him. One finds preserved in Little Italies all over the world customs and rituals which have long fallen into disuse in Italy. By its very nature Little Italy is a kind of reliquary of habits that are no longer relevant. One of the wonderful things about the book called *Immigrants: A Portrait of the Urban Experience 1890-1930*, by Robert Harney and Harold Troper[14] is that it captures the stasis, the resistance to change within the walls I have been referring to. The faces that stare out at us from the photographs are frozen in those expressions for all eternity. In real life, change inevitably comes.

Perhaps now we are in a position to define Italian-Canadian writing. It is a body of literature in English, French, and Italian produced by writers who have at least one parent of Italian origin. These writers are, almost without exception, the second generation, the children of parents who made the decision to emigrate. They are mostly young — very few are over forty. Their work treats certain themes which characterize it as Italo-Canadian, the most prominent of which is a sense of "wandering between two worlds, one dead/the other powerless to be born." Clustered about this central theme are others like relationships within the family, generally between parents and children; nostalgia for an idealized past in Italy; a return to Italy which results in the conviction that Canada is home after all; a rejection of ethnic stereotypes as impediments to true integration; and a confrontation with death as older relatives die far away in the old country without their children beside them or parents die in Canada far from the land of their birth. The death theme inevitably also implies the death of a way of life.

It is necessary to define Italian-Canadian literature thematically in order to give the term any meaning at all. It is literature which touches both Italy and Canada. To expand it to include all literature written by people of Italian origin is, I think, to turn it into a mere "geographical hypothesis."[15]

A consequence of narrowing the definition of Italian-Canadian literature in this way is that we are left with what is in reality a fleeting phenomenon. No writer can remain fixated on his origins for very long, especially when those origins are in a country far away and a culture very different from the one he is living and working in. As the Montreal poet Mario Campo remarks, "Il est futile de rester accrocher au passé; il faut cesser de regarder constamment en arrière."[16] The Italo-Canadian writers tend to spend a period of time early in their careers confronting the fact of their immigration and totting up the balance sheet of its gains and losses. Then one of two things happens. Some simply stop writing. For them the act of writing has been an outlet, a way of resolving the angst associated with their transplantation. Once the conflict is resolved, they no longer need the therapy, as it were, and we do not hear from them any more. Others continue to write, but Italy and the other themes I detailed above simply recede to the margins of their pages.

It is for this reason that I prefer to speak of Italo-Canadian literature rather than Italo-Canadian writers. I think there comes a point when the prefix is no longer appropriate for the writers. Italo-Canadian writing is circumscribed by time. It is the product of a moment in a writer's life, and that moment vanishes.

Some continue to write after the Italo-Canadian stage has worn itself out, and these we simply call Canadian writers. It is not that they cease to be of Italian origin. But they carry that heritage with them the way other Canadians carry the fact that they come from Toronto rather than Vancouver or a farm rather than a city. Italy filters through in past tenses; their present is Canadian.

NOTES

1. Susanna Moodie, *Roughing It in the Bush* (Toronto, reprint edition, 1970).

2. Mario Duliani, *La ville sans femmes* (Montréal, 1945). Duliani translated it into Italian and republished it the following year under the title *La Città Senza Donne*.

3. Moodie, *Roughing*, 237.

4. Duliani, *Ville*, 91.

5. The reference is to the corner of Dufferin Street and St. Clair Avenue in the heart of Toronto's Little Italy. The poem appears in the anthology Pier Giorgio Di Cicco ed. *Roman Candles* (Toronto, 1978), 81. Further references to this collection will be identified in the text by the letters "*RC*" followed by a page number.

6. *Quaderni Canadesi* 3 (1978), 4.

7. In the *Journal of Canadian Fiction* 3 (1974), 23.

8. "Mimosa," *Mimosa and Other Poems* (Oakville, Ont., 1981), 12.

9. *Ibid.*, 16.

10. Frank Paci, *The Italians* (Scarborough, Ont., 1978); *Black Madonna* (Ottawa, 1982); *The Father* (Ottawa, 1984).

11. Marco Micone, *Gens du silence* (Montréal, 1982).

12. Filippo Salvatore, *La Fresque de Mussolini* (Montréal, 1985).

13. Paci, *Father*, 69.

14. Robert Harney and Harold Troper, *Immigrants: A Portrait of the Urban Experience 1890-1930* (Toronto, 1975).

15. The phrase appears in Joe Pivato's poem, "Cultura Canadese," *RC*, 81.

16. *Coma Laudanum* (Montréal, 1979).

Italo-Canadian Poetry and Ethnic Semiosis in the Postmodern Context

William Boelhower

I have chosen to insert my discussion of Italo-Canadian poetry in the larger context of ethnic semiosis in the post-modern episteme for reasons crucial to an understanding of the type of poetry (and poetics) exemplified in the anthology *Roman Candles*, edited by Pier Giorgio Di Cicco.[1] There is a level at which the anthology's individual poems, when taken as a single macrotext, recount a story that is common to all of them. It is this documentary level that appears least incidental and best suited to the task of clarifying the conceptual limits and possibilities of the individual poems.[2] It might be called, roughly, the story behind the poems, the one all the poems are implicitly trying to tell, or more specifically, the level at which one is confronted with the narration of the attempt to work out an ethnic poetics. If we take *Roman Candles* as our text, then surely the very possibility of generating ethnic discourse becomes the pre-text.

Indeed, if one pushes each poem in this collection to its limits, one is inevitably faced with the larger and shared issue of ethnic semiosis, at the centre of which lies the very act of producing the ethnic sign and of constructing the ethnic subject as author and cultural protagonist. But judging from the poems themselves, the possibilities of inserting such ethnic poetry in the total context of its own model of ethnic semiosis are rare, due to a cultural politics of a centring and centralized order of official discourse. In fact, as users of an "unofficial language" (Di Cicco's words in the Preface) and as generators of a decentring ethnic semiosis, Italo-Canadian poets are naturally enough marginal to an interpretative order of cultural nationalism which Di Cicco calls "Canadianism," and which leads to the ethnopoetic condition of a "displaced sensibility."[3] This is why, I presume, Italo-Canadian literature is a literature still fighting for cultural status and why it is of crucial importance to clarify the semiotic programme, the pre-text, by means of which the ethnic poet and his/her model reader may meet.

Needless to say, ethnic poetry is often considered culturally poor because of the poverty of its interpreter or his lack of fluency in the type of local semiosis that accounts for the ethnic subject and ethnic poetics. Far from being trapped in a pathetic anthropology that can at best promote a nostalgic quest for lost roots and existential wholeness, Italo-Canadian poets have provided a radical critique of the postmodern condition in Canada by relying on what can be called the micro-strategies of ethnic sign production. The rest of my paper, therefore, will deal with a description of the cultural model behind the production of Italo-Canadian poetry.

The Topological Scheme

In his preface to *Roman Candles*, Pier Giorgio Di Cicco sums up his return voyage to Italy in this way: "I went out of curiosity, and came back to Canada conscious of the fact that I'd been a man without a country for most of my life" (p. 9). In her poem "Enigmatico" Mary di Michele expresses this condition even more dramatically (p. 62):

> and she cries out caught
> with one bare foot in a village in the Abruzzi,
> the other busy with cramped English speaking toes
> in Toronto,
> she strides the Atlantic legs spread
> like a Colossus.

The modality of di Michele's "striding" and the sense of radical dislocation expressed by Di Cicco point to a geographical strategy that suggests an aesthetics of spatial juxtaposition. In fact, ethnic semiosis is ultimately organized on the basis of a topological system that generates an open series of such binary categories as Old World/New World; emigrant/immigrant; ethnic/non-ethnic; presence/absence; origin/traces; continuity/discontinuity; orientation/disorientation; dwelling/nomadism; house/road; centre/periphery; proximity/distance. This chronotopic system provides not only a way of seeing but also a way of thinking that has its own type of *savoir-faire*. Its perspectival mechanism is stereoscopic and suggests how the ethnic subject proceeds in creating ethnic space within Canadian culture. For example, in Joseph Pivato's poem "Alberta S.P.Q.R." there is this tensional strategy (p. 78):

Arno, Brenta, Po, Tagliamento
  no Lombardy poplars
  Canadian aspens
  reach up to
  a babelled horizon.

In reality, however, this ethnic space is essentially a hyperspace, a hermeneutical nowhere and everywhere in which the ethnic subject floats between two worlds, two cultural models. The type of space I am referring to is the particular space of ethnic semiosis.

What is more, there is a strong degree of reversibility implied in the subject's being "between" that simultaneously permits both acts of conjunction and disjunction, ranging from Joseph Pivato's "First-Born Son" (p. 79) to the desperate words "(N.B. I am without a country, speechless.)" of Mary Melfi's poem "The Wanderer" (p. 64). Given this copresence of cultural models and the principle of reversibility deriving from it, the ethnic subject is able to carry out his/her *jeu* of ambivalence, break up the unidirectionality of official cultural discourse and unscrew the signifiers bolted down to established codes. In short, this self is ready to create semantic disorder, and, through the production of a semantic excess, shortcircuit discourse based on fixed equivalences and the principle of non-contradiction. "That woman is either walking backwards or forwards," Melfi writes in "The Exile" (p. 63). And in the second poem of his sequence "Three Poems for Giovanni Caboto," Filippo Salvatore asks Cabot (p. 14):

Where are you looking to?
Towards the new or the old world?
You don't answer me, of course,

you remain standing at Atwater and
keep on gazing afar.

Such a practice of ethnic interrogation as this, and one finds it operating throughout the collection of *Roman Candles*, refuses to reduce the order of discourse to a single meaning, a single code or cultural model and prefers instead a strategy of perspectival ambiguity. We are, in other words, in the midst of an economy of ethnic con-fusion (συηβάλλεἰν), of symbolic discourse.[4]

The Genealogical Principle

Before relating this economy to an Italo-Canadian poetics and the latter to certain features of postmodernism, I must briefly try to outline the other necessary components that characterize ethnic semiosis in general. The very type of symbolic discourse which ethnic semiosis generates is fundamentally an expression of the quest for a *patria*, for a dwelling.[5] Within the context of its special topological system described above, ethnic discourse clearly tries, and is conscious of trying, to recompose the binary polarities deriving from its spatial sense. That is why, for example, ethnic poetry often resorts to a highly narrative syntax, not because it eliminates the negative categories of the binary polarities or abandons the aesthetics of juxtaposition, but because it uses the positive categories as part of its project of refounding the negative ones. Of course we are talking about the symbolic space of ethnic poetics, and on a broader level about ethnic semiosis, and it is perhaps the only space where these binary categories can be treated dialectically — or, in the extreme case, in utopian terms of allegorical inversion. The concept of the project (of projecting a possible world) and consequently the ethnic subject's confidence in narrativity are expressed in Filippo Salavatore's poem "My War" as "my fight" for "the just/dimension between man and the world" (p. 23). But the ethnic aggressivity of the poem's narrative voice is knowingly based on "my patrimony in a cheap, pasteboard suitcase" (p. 22).

The suitcase itself is a virtual text of the immigrant process of radical dislocation. What one would find in it were one at the customs office in the guise of a semiotic inspector is nothing other than the genealogical principle basic to any ethnic discourse, but also to writing characterized by Roman Jakobson's notion of contiguity. In Italo-Canadian poetry this principle is often inscribed tellurically in the Italian landscape as cultural memory; in which case "All the world is a village lost/in time, suspended/in space" and the very notion of an originating place becomes a "stop watch of human/memory" (see di Michele's poem "Across the Atlantic," p. 60), a version of Solomon's sword for judging between our topologically generated polarities. Genealogy can also be expressed as "Il Sangue," as it is in Len Gasparini's homonymous poem where "The blood that moves through your language/moves through mine" (p. 26). It is on the strength of this ethnic pulse beat that Gasparini can calmly state, "The city's iron skyline/bends before the structure of a poem" (pp. 26-7). Once again the bloodlink of language flows back to an originating source, to "Our people" who "work in the Tuscan fields" (p. 27), a genealogical source that opens an ethno-symbolic space in which the far is made near and the near far.

The Politics of Memory

I think it is now evident that the project of ethnic semiosis, its ability to *raccontare*, is also essentially an epistemological exercise in remembering. Put in another way, its model of *vedere* is an act of interrogating, through mnemotechnical strategies, various versions of the past considered as a temporal-spatial construct. The semiotic dynamic at work here can be expressed as follows:

$$\text{MEMORY} \leftrightarrows \text{PROJECT.}$$

It is within this cultural cathode tube that genealogical discourse is charted. There can be no project without memory and without a project memory has no coherence, as much of postmodern poetics surely proves. It is not surprising, therefore, that the mnemotechnical strategies, the rhetorical tropes of memory, used in the majority of the poems in *Roman Candles* take the form of recalling and interpreting old photographs, funerals and wakes, the calm gaze of grandparents, the defeat of immigrant fathers, and old-world place as an *umbilicus mundi*. In his poem "Archeology," in which the project of identity is founded on old-world geography as the locus of memory, Tony Pignataro says, "This is the inheritance of sons; / to be rooted in their father's faith. / To rediscover hewn stone" (p. 50). In a poem entitled "Memento d'Italia" Di Cicco's narrator journeys to Italy "to learn images unrazed" and by poem's end can state (p. 35):

> This I brought back with me.
> An affirmation.
> Much that went between this man [immigrant father]
> and I is changed.

Here not only is geography a memory system and memory geographical (or "Tutto il mondo e paese," as Mary di Michele would have it in "Across the Atlantic"), but the ethnic self very consciously and obsessively assumes the role of son or daughter. This too is a genealogical stance, only now the constructive device is generational, even if the quest for continuity through a politics of memory is obviously the same. The point is, being a son or daughter within the topological scheme of ethnic semiosis implies a unique way of organizing experience and formulating a possible world. The ethnic subject, I repeat, measures himself/herself according to the circumstances of topology, the originating parameters of which were set down by the voyage of the emigrant/immigrant generation. Thus the subject produces ethnic semiosis through a strategic use of memory which is nothing other than the intensive and extensive interrogation of the originating project of a founding generation. The ethnic subject goes forward by going backwards. It is this kind of questioning that produces an ethnic *savoir-faire*, both as competence and performance.[6]

The Postmodern Context

Now the need to define the place of ethnic semiosis in the postmodern context should seem imperative, for ethnic poetics, as is often thought, has little to do with a literal return or a mere repetition of elements called up from an already achieved cultural storehouse. To think otherwise is to deny tensional status to the ethnic *verbum*, to rob it of its specific difference, to domesticate its peculiar ambivalence through a system of reassuring cultural equivalences.

In fact, we are not dealing here with a mimetic poetics, which would result in touristic and even voyeuristic modes of representation not unlike those of folkloric revivalism. Instead, ethnic representation lies in the *production* of identity through ethnic interpretation, which is made possible only through the ethnic subject's decision to stride two cultural systems. In other words, it is not a question of attributing a lost substance or metaphysical *Grund* to the ethnic self; but of metaphorically floating a series of culturally weak identifications through a disjunctive/conjunctive *jeu* of ethnic ambiguity. Thus, in this context what may be intentionally read as a simple strategy of retotalization is actually (within the perspective of ethnic semiosis) a strategy of producing a specific difference in the domain of the official culture. And the ethnic subject produces difference by thinking differently, that is, by questioning the original project of the immigrant fathers and mothers. In effect, ethnic semiosis as *poiesis* means recounting a rival story, what we might call a mapping exercise in ethnic tracing, an attempt to recount a series of micro-differences.

The original, foundational project is, of course, an absent presence, or there would be no need for the supplementary strategy of ethnic interpretation; indeed, the founding subject (the immigrant generation) is by definition out of place, the founding project so many scattered clues. That this is the peculiar condition in which ethnic semiosis operates is evident in Mary Melfi's poem "The Wanderer" where she observes, "We are all citizens of make-believe" (p. 64). It is not a question of mere continuism or of an act of literal reconstruction, therefore, but a question of generating micro-sequences of ethnic continuity within a broader context of discontinuity. One "can't make a living from tradition" (p. 44), Antonio

Iacovino notes in "You Went to the Big Festivity." Saro D'Agostino clarifies the epistemologically weak status of the Italo-Canadian poetic *verbum* when he says, "my father suffered more/indignities than words/could ever dream/of conjuring" — "Father/I am sorry for these songs" (p. 71). In "Cultura Canadese" Pivato's poet cries out, "where is our history in this land?" (p. 81) In short, it is precisely through the act of creating the ethnic sign that the Italo-Canadian poet places himself/herself momentarily outside and beyond the reach of a totalizing order of cultural discourse. I say "momentarily" simply because at this point the ethnic self is caught in a double bind; knowing as he/she does that the very discourse he/she uses to criticize postmodern Canadian culture is itself subject to a larger order of discourse. In other words, while ethnic semiosis can produce an infinite and uncontrollable (because deterritorialized) series of micro-discourse events, it cannot rebuild its own cultural paradigm. There is no refoundation. We are now necessarily faced with the status of ethnic semiosis in a postmodern context.

Apart from the justified quarrel over the unfortunate choice of the term "postmodernism," I think we can agree on a set of characteristics that help to circumscribe contemporary experience. One is certainly the fact that the old legitimizing macro-discourse systems (such as Marxism, Darwinianism and Freudianism) are no longer valid comprehensive paradigms; and resulting from this cultural state of affairs and from the fact that we now live in a technotronic mass-media society, it seems that the very notion of the modernist self has been reduced to a mere metaphor, to a set of simulated performances.[7] Furthermore, when Pivato asks in his poem "Cultura Canadese" "is this a paese/or a geographical hypothesis?" I think he has grasped the essential feature of contemporary reality in which it is no longer possible to dwell in the traditional sense of dwelling in the polis. All the negative categories pertaining to the topological scheme of ethnic semiosis are, it seems, attributable to life in the postmodern habitat. Of course, such categories as discontinuity and nomadism and radical change can be interpreted positively in the sense that the availability of a plurality of simulated scenarios allows the metropolitan self to switch from one possible world to another with unthinking ease. And this floating version of subjectivity suggests that, at least for the present, an open series of micro-strategies (getting along from day to day) can suffice to create an apparently free subject.

What seems missing from this postmodern frame, however, is exactly a politics of memory which, as we have seen, characterizes the semiotic program of the ethnic subject and which, indeed, allows him/her to define and deconstruct the very categories that make up the postmodern condition. I do not mean that the ethnic subject can escape this condition, but, through ethnic semiosis, he/she is surely in a privileged position to interpret it and include it within a larger self-reflexive *jeu*. Quite frankly, is not this one of the reasons why ethnicity has become such a popular, not to say explosive filter for questioning the very foundations of the way in which contemporary experience is organized? As a form of cultural politics and as an interpretative model, ethnicity has performed open-heart surgery on advanced post-industrial society and knows there is no heart to speak of. Through its mnemotechnical strategies and its use of genealogy as an alternative ordering principle, ethnic semiosis offers a double perspective of postmodern identity. "Ah, God, are they not our families, without/a place to go back to what will be our lives!'' Antonino Mazza writes in ''Death in Italy'' (p. 40). In such instances ethnic reflexivity tends to historicize the agenerational and atemporal condition of the present. Indeed, in a culture without a historical memory, where the crisis of identity and the crisis of memory are coterminous, remembering is itself the ethnic project. By interrogating the genealogical gaze of the parents and their *traditio*, the ethnic subject opens up a new inferencing field and constructs a different interpretation of cultural facts.

Of course, the ethnic poet knows it is impossible to escape the radical condition of discontinuity he/she finds oneself in. Indeed, this condition is a constitutive part of the topological scheme that generates the ethnic sign. As Alexandre Amprimoz writes (p. 76):

Hubert, pauvre Hubert,
il n'y aura plus de Prochain Épisode...
All images are political,
there is no refuge,
no Bohemian Embassy for poets.

But it is exactly at this point that the ethnic *jeu* begins, as a micro-strategic exercise in cultural politics, in producing brief eruptive moments of ethnic difference. Outside of his interpretative act, the ethnic subject may even slip back into anonymity and be swallowed up by the larger culture. This ethnic circumstance of optional or symbolic identification is captured by Filippo Salvatore in one of his poems on Giovanni Caboto (p. 16):

The life
of your memory is as ethereal for me

as this early morning-sun,
as my lucidity...
People continue to come out [of the Metro],
become a crowd that
snakes me up, clogs me, carries me away.

Although unseen, the ethnic self sees all. Paradoxically, even if in this culturally weak position — like Len Gasparini's "Marginal Man" "trying to survive/My environment.../Buried deepest in the work I love" (p. 25) —, the ethnic subject is semiotically strong because of the special status of the originating cultural *traditio* which, as an absent presence, solicits ethnic interpretation in a metacultural space that is nowhere and everywhere at the same time. As Michel Serres says, knowledge of foundations is founded on a tomb.[8] In "Nostalgia" Di Cicco writes (p. 32):

under a few cold lilies, my father dreams
cicadas in vallemaio. I am sure of it,
he left me that, and a poem that is only a

dream of cicadas....

Here memory as project is quite explicit, and where this floating strategy leads to, Di Cicco suggests at the end of the poem: "I am a little marvellous, with the sunken/heart of exiles" (p. 33).

If this symbolic vantage point occupies a minimal cultural space, still it can in no way be monitored or controlled, for the ethnic sign is dispersive, supplementary, polymorphic, the result of a contradictory and ambivalent "betweenness." Being dislocated, the ethnic subject's semiosis is often a mere factor of disorder or excess, a mere act of interpretation or questioning. But the competence of producing ethnic discourse in the context sketched above is spelled out brilliantly in Di Cicco's poem "Remembering Baltimore, Arezzo" (p. 37):

> I am not alone, I have never been alone. Ghosts
> are barking
> in my eyes, their soft tears washing us down to
> baltimore, out the chesapeake, round the atlantic,
> round the world,
> back where we started from, a small town in the
> shade of cypress, with nowhere to go but be still again.

Here the genealogical project, the politics of memory, the double perspectivism of the subject are all operating, and as ethnic he is both everywhere and nowhere (his originating ghosts having become floating, disincarnated traces). But the poem goes even further to clarify the particular *jeu* of ethnic self-reflexivity and its subversive status:

> It is a way of saying twenty-five years
> and some german bombs have made for roses in
> a backyard that
> we cry over, like some film which is too maudlin
> to pity
> and yet is the best we have to feel human about.

There is no totalizing strategy in these lines, only a kind of semiotic challenge in a minor genealogical key. There is also an originating source of difference here which is, of course, the tomb of the immigrant father, and it not only precedes but makes possible the poet-son's act of reflection. Ethnic semiosis, then, is a way of thinking differently by thinking the difference, and in the postmodern framework this may be all the difference there is: a particular form of waiting, of holding one's ground. It is fitting to conclude now with these words from Antonino Mazza's poem "Our House Is in a Cosmic Ear" (p. 42):

> if the dream doesn't stop, if the word,
> if the house
> is in the word and we, by chance, should meet,
> my house is your house, take it.

NOTES

1. Pier Giorgio Di Cicco, ed. *Roman Candles* (Toronto, 1978).

2. For a further discussion of the concept "documentary level," *cf.* Kurt H. Wolff, ed., *From Karl Mannheim* (New York, 1971), 30-38. Briefly, it is at this level that one can delineate the objective possibilities, the structural horizon, within which the Italo-Canadian experience takes shape, whether consciously or not is here beside the point.

3. *Roman Candles*, 9. Subsequent page references to the poems in this anthology will henceforth be included in my text.

4. For a further explication of sign con-fusion as I intend it here, *cf.* Umberto Galimberti, *Il corpo* (Milan, 1983), 239-47.

5. *Cf.* Martin Heidegger's essay "Building Dwelling Thinking," Françoise Choay, dir., *L'urbanisme. Utopies et réalités* (Paris, 1965); Francesco Dal Co, *Abitare nel moderno* (Bari, 1983).

6. I am referring here to the theory of modal analysis developed by A.J. Greimas, *Du Sens II* (Paris, 1983), 67-102.

7. *Cf.* Jean-François Lyotard, *La condizione postmoderna*, trans. into Italian by Carlo Formenti (Milan, 1981); Gianni Vattimo, *Al di là del soggetto* (Milan, 1981); Mario Perniola, *La società dei simulacra* (Bologna, 1980).

8. Michel Serres, "Introduzione a 'Rome' di Michel Serres," *aut aut*, nos. 197-98 (September-December, 1983), 3.

Name Index

The *Essay* Series of Guernica

1. *Contrasts: Comparative Essays on Italian-Canadian Writing*. Edited by Joseph Pivato.
2. *The Courage of Poetry* by Paul Chamberland
3. *Gramsci's Political Thought* by Jean-Marc Piotte (forthcoming)
4. *Antichi e Moderni in Italia nel Seicento* by Filippo Salvatore
6. *Writers in Transition*: The Proceedings of the First National Conference of Italian-Canadian Writers. Edited by C.D. Minni and Anna Coschi Ciampolini.
7. *Arrangiarsi: The Italian Immigration Experience in Canada*. Edited by Roberto Perin and Franc Sturino
8. *Le cinéma aujourd'hui: Films, théories, nouvelles approches*. Sous la direction de Michel Larouche.

Achevé d'imprimer
en janvier 1989 sur les presses
des Ateliers Graphiques Marc Veilleux Inc.
Cap-Saint-Ignace, Qué.